Mental Health Act 2007

CHAPTER 12

Explanatory Notes are available separately

GRAN*GIS* UK Publishing

Adapted and published by GRANGIS (Grand Register Library).
Online: www.grangis.com
E-mail: contact@grangis.com

In this version:
ISBN: 979-8-88559-028-0

Note: This is the original version (as it was originally enacted). Title, sub-title and the generated date is as marked on the pages.

Mental Health Act 2007

CHAPTER 12

MENTAL HEALTH ACT 2007

PART 1

AMENDMENTS TO MENTAL HEALTH ACT 1983

CHAPTER 1

CHANGES TO KEY PROVISIONS

Mental disorder

Tests for detention etc

Medical treatment

Fundamental principles

CHAPTER 2

PROFESSIONAL ROLES

Approved clinicians and responsible clinicians

Approved mental health professionals

Conflicts of interest in professional roles

CHAPTER 3

SAFEGUARDS FOR PATIENTS

Patient's nearest relative

Consent to treatment

Advocacy

Accommodation, etc.

CHAPTER 4

SUPERVISED COMMUNITY TREATMENT

CHAPTER 5

MENTAL HEALTH REVIEW TRIBUNALS

CHAPTER 6

CROSS-BORDER PATIENTS

CHAPTER 7

RESTRICTED PATIENTS

CHAPTER 8

MISCELLANEOUS

PART 2

AMENDMENTS TO OTHER ACTS

CHAPTER 1

AMENDMENTS TO DOMESTIC VIOLENCE, CRIME AND VICTIMS ACT 2004

CHAPTER 2

AMENDMENTS TO MENTAL CAPACITY ACT 2005

PART 3

GENERAL

SCHEDULES

Mental Health Act 2007

2007 CHAPTER 12

An Act to amend the Mental Health Act 1983, the Domestic Violence, Crime and Victims Act 2004 and the Mental Capacity Act 2005 in relation to mentally disordered persons; to amend section 40 of the Mental Capacity Act 2005; and for connected purposes. [19th July 2007]

BE IT ENACTED by the Queen's most Excellent Majesty, by and with the advice and consent of the Lords Spiritual and Temporal, and Commons, in this present Parliament assembled, and by the authority of the same, as follows:—

PART 1

AMENDMENTS TO MENTAL HEALTH ACT 1983

CHAPTER 1

CHANGES TO KEY PROVISIONS

Mental disorder

1 Removal of categories of mental disorder

(1) Section 1(2) of the 1983 Act (key definitions) is amended as set out in subsections (2) and (3).

(2) For the definitions of "mental disorder" and "mentally disordered" substitute—

""mental disorder" means any disorder or disability of the mind; and

"mentally disordered" shall be construed accordingly;".

(3) The following definitions are omitted—

(a) those of "severe mental impairment" and "severely mentally impaired",
(b) those of "mental impairment" and "mentally impaired", and
(c) that of "psychopathic disorder".

(4) Schedule 1 (which contains further amendments to the 1983 Act and amendments to other Acts) has effect.

2 Learning disability

(1) Section 1 of the 1983 Act (application of Act) is amended as follows.

(2) After subsection (2) insert—

"(2A) But a person with learning disability shall not be considered by reason of that disability to be—
(a) suffering from mental disorder for the purposes of the provisions mentioned in subsection (2B) below; or
(b) requiring treatment in hospital for mental disorder for the purposes of sections 17E and 50 to 53 below,

unless that disability is associated with abnormally aggressive or seriously irresponsible conduct on his part.

(2B) The provisions are—
(a) sections 3, 7, 17A, 20 and 20A below;
(b) sections 35 to 38, 45A, 47, 48 and 51 below; and
(c) section 72(1)(b) and (c) and (4) below."

(3) After subsection (3) insert—

"(4) In subsection (2A) above, "learning disability" means a state of arrested or incomplete development of the mind which includes significant impairment of intelligence and social functioning."

3 Changes to exclusions from operation of 1983 Act

In section 1 of the 1983 Act (application of Act), for subsection (3) substitute—

"(3) Dependence on alcohol or drugs is not considered to be a disorder or disability of the mind for the purposes of subsection (2) above."

Tests for detention etc

4 Replacement of "treatability" and "care" tests with appropriate treatment test

(1) The 1983 Act is amended as follows.

(2) In section 3 (admission for treatment)—
(a) in subsection (2), omit paragraph (b) (and the word "and" at the end of that paragraph),
(b) in that subsection, after paragraph (c) insert "; and
(d) appropriate medical treatment is available for him.", and
(c) in subsection (3)(a), for "(b)" substitute "(d)".

(3) In that section, after subsection (3) insert—

"(4) In this Act, references to appropriate medical treatment, in relation to a person suffering from mental disorder, are references to medical treatment which is appropriate in his case, taking into account the nature and degree of the mental disorder and all other circumstances of his case."

(4) In section 20 (renewal of authority to detain), in subsection (4)—

(a) omit paragraph (b) (and the word "and" at the end of that paragraph),

(b) after paragraph (c) insert "and

(d) appropriate medical treatment is available for him.", and

(c) omit the words from "but, in the case of mental illness" to the end.

(5) In section 37(2) (conditions for exercise of powers of court to order hospital admission or guardianship), in paragraph (a)(i), for the words from ", in the case of psychopathic disorder" to the end substitute "appropriate medical treatment is available for him; or".

(6) In section 45A(2) (conditions for exercise of powers of court to direct hospital admission), for paragraph (c) substitute—

"(c) that appropriate medical treatment is available for him."

(7) In section 47(1) (conditions for exercise of Secretary of State's powers to direct removal to hospital), in paragraph (b), for the words from "and, in the case of psychopathic disorder" to the end substitute "; and

(c) that appropriate medical treatment is available for him;".

(8) In section 72—

(a) in subsection (1)(b) (powers of tribunal to direct discharge of patient not liable to be detained under section 2), after sub-paragraph (ii) insert—

"(iia) that appropriate medical treatment is available for him; or", and

(b) omit subsection (2).

(9) In section 73(1) (powers of tribunal to direct discharge of restricted patients), in paragraph (a), for "or (ii)" substitute ", (ii) or (iia)".

(10) In section 145 (interpretation), after subsection (1AA) insert—

"(1AB) References in this Act to appropriate medical treatment shall be construed in accordance with section 3(4) above."

5 Further cases in which appropriate treatment test is to apply

(1) The 1983 Act is amended as follows.

(2) In section 36(1) (remand to hospital for treatment) after paragraph (a) (inserted by Schedule 1 to this Act) insert "and

(b) appropriate medical treatment is available for him."

(3) In section 48(1) (removal to hospital of immigration detainees etc) after paragraph (b) (inserted by Schedule 1 to this Act) insert "and

(c) appropriate medical treatment is available for him;".

(4) In section 51(6)(a) (further power to make hospital order) after sub-paragraph (i) (inserted by Schedule 1 to this Act) insert "and

(ii) appropriate medical treatment is available for him; and".

Medical treatment

6 Appropriate treatment test in Part 4 of 1983 Act

(1) Part 4 of the 1983 Act (consent to treatment) is amended as follows.

(2) In the following provisions, for the words from ", having regard to" to the end substitute "it is appropriate for the treatment to be given."—

(a) section 57(2)(b) (certification of second opinion where treatment requires consent and a second opinion), and

(b) section 58(3)(b) (certification of second opinion where treatment requires consent or a second opinion).

(3) In section 64 (supplementary provisions for Part 4), after subsection (2) insert—

"(3) For the purposes of this Part of this Act, it is appropriate for treatment to be given to a patient if the treatment is appropriate in his case, taking into account the nature and degree of the mental disorder from which he is suffering and all other circumstances of his case."

7 Change in definition of "medical treatment"

(1) Section 145 of the 1983 Act is amended as follows.

(2) In subsection (1), in the definition of "medical treatment", for the words from "and also" to the end substitute "psychological intervention and specialist mental health habilitation, rehabilitation and care (but see also subsection (4) below);".

(3) After subsection (3) insert—

"(4) Any reference in this Act to medical treatment, in relation to mental disorder, shall be construed as a reference to medical treatment the purpose of which is to alleviate, or prevent a worsening of, the disorder or one or more of its symptoms or manifestations."

Fundamental principles

8 The fundamental principles

After section 118(2) of the 1983 Act (code of practice) insert—

"(2A) The code shall include a statement of the principles which the Secretary of State thinks should inform decisions under this Act.

(2B) In preparing the statement of principles the Secretary of State shall, in particular, ensure that each of the following matters is addressed—

(a) respect for patients' past and present wishes and feelings,

(b) respect for diversity generally including, in particular, diversity of religion, culture and sexual orientation (within the meaning of section 35 of the Equality Act 2006),

(c) minimising restrictions on liberty,

(d) involvement of patients in planning, developing and delivering care and treatment appropriate to them,

(e) avoidance of unlawful discrimination,

(f) effectiveness of treatment,

(g) views of carers and other interested parties,

(h) patient wellbeing and safety, and

(i) public safety.

(2C) The Secretary of State shall also have regard to the desirability of ensuring—

(a) the efficient use of resources, and

(b) the equitable distribution of services.

(2D) In performing functions under this Act persons mentioned in subsection (1)(a) or (b) shall have regard to the code."

CHAPTER 2

PROFESSIONAL ROLES

Approved clinicians and responsible clinicians

9 Amendments to Part 2 of 1983 Act

(1) Part 2 of the 1983 Act (compulsory admission to hospital and guardianship) is amended as follows.

(2) In section 5 (application in respect of patient already in hospital)—

(a) in subsection (2), after "registered medical practitioner" insert "or approved clinician",

(b) for subsection (3) substitute—

"(3) The registered medical practitioner or approved clinician in charge of the treatment of a patient in a hospital may nominate one (but not more than one) person to act for him under subsection (2) above in his absence.

(3A) For the purposes of subsection (3) above—

(a) the registered medical practitioner may nominate another registered medical practitioner, or an approved clinician, on the staff of the hospital; and

(b) the approved clinician may nominate another approved clinician, or a registered medical practitioner, on the staff of the hospital.", and

(c) in subsection (4), after "a practitioner", in each place, insert "or clinician".

(3) In section 17 (leave of absence)—

(a) in subsection (1)—
   (i) for "responsible medical officer" substitute "responsible clinician", and
   (ii) for "that officer" substitute "that clinician",
(b) in subsection (3), for "responsible medical officer" substitute "responsible clinician", and
(c) in subsection (4)—
   (i) for "responsible medical officer" substitute "responsible clinician", and
   (ii) for "that officer" substitute "that clinician".

(4) In section 20 (duration of authority)—
(a) in subsections (3) and (5), for "responsible medical officer" substitute "responsible clinician",
(b) after subsection (5) insert—

"(5A) But the responsible clinician may not furnish a report under subsection (3) above unless a person—
(a) who has been professionally concerned with the patient's medical treatment; but
(b) who belongs to a profession other than that to which the responsible clinician belongs,

states in writing that he agrees that the conditions set out in subsection (4) above are satisfied.",
(c) in subsection (6), for "appropriate medical officer" substitute "appropriate practitioner", and
(d) omit subsection (10).

(5) In section 21B (patients who are taken into custody or return after more than 28 days) —
(a) in subsections (2) and (3), for "appropriate medical officer" substitute "appropriate practitioner", and
(b) in subsection (10), omit the definition of "appropriate medical officer".

(6) In section 23(2) (persons who may apply for discharge of patient), in paragraphs (a) and (b), for "responsible medical officer" substitute "responsible clinician".

(7) In section 24 (visiting and examination of patients), in each place, after "registered medical practitioner" insert "or approved clinician".

(8) In section 25(1) (restrictions on discharge by nearest relative)—
(a) for "responsible medical officer" substitute "responsible clinician", and
(b) for "that officer" substitute "that clinician".

(9) In section 34 (interpretation of Part 2 of the 1983 Act), in subsection (1), insert the following definition at the appropriate place—

""the appropriate practitioner" means—
(a) in the case of a patient who is subject to the guardianship of a person other than a local social services authority, the nominated medical attendant of the patient; and
(b) in any other case, the responsible clinician;".

(10) In that subsection, for the definition of "the responsible medical officer" substitute—

""the responsible clinician" means—

(a) in relation to a patient liable to be detained by virtue of an application for admission for assessment or an application for admission for treatment, or a community patient, the approved clinician with overall responsibility for the patient's case;

(b) in relation to a patient subject to guardianship, the approved clinician authorised by the responsible local social services authority to act (either generally or in any particular case or for any particular purpose) as the responsible clinician;".

10 Amendments to Part 3 of 1983 Act

(1) Part 3 of the 1983 Act (patients concerned in criminal proceedings) is amended as follows.

(2) In section 35 (remand to hospital for report)—

(a) in subsections (4) and (5), for "registered medical practitioner" substitute "approved clinician", and

(b) in subsection (8), after "registered medical practitioner" insert "or approved clinician".

(3) In section 36 (remand to hospital for treatment)—

(a) in subsection (3), for "registered medical practitioner who would be in charge of his treatment" substitute "approved clinician who would have overall responsibility for his case",

(b) in subsection (4), for "responsible medical officer" substitute "responsible clinician", and

(c) in subsection (7), after "registered medical practitioner" insert "or approved clinician".

(4) In section 37 (hospital and guardianship orders), in subsection (4), for "registered medical practitioner who would be in charge of his treatment" substitute "approved clinician who would have overall responsibility for his case".

(5) In section 38 (interim hospital orders)—

(a) in subsection (4), for "registered medical practitioner who would be in charge of his treatment" substitute "approved clinician who would have overall responsibility for his case", and

(b) in subsection (5), for "responsible medical officer", in each place, substitute "responsible clinician".

(6) In section 41 (power of courts to restrict discharge from hospital), in subsections (3)(c) and (6), for "responsible medical officer" substitute "responsible clinician".

(7) In section 44(2) (person who is to give evidence in connection with committal to hospital), for "registered medical practitioner who would be in charge of the offender's treatment" substitute "approved clinician who would have overall responsibility for the offender's case".

(8) In section 45A(5) (person who is to give evidence in connection with hospital or limitation direction), for "registered medical practitioner who would be in charge of

his treatment" substitute "approved clinician who would have overall responsibility for his case".

(9) In the following provisions, for "responsible medical officer" substitute "responsible clinician"—

(a) section 45B(3) (requirement to produce report on person subject to hospital and limitation directions), and

(b) section 49(3) (requirement to produce report on person subject to restriction direction).

11 Further amendments to Part 3 of 1983 Act

(1) Part 3 of the 1983 Act (patients concerned in criminal proceedings) is further amended as follows.

(2) In section 50(1) (powers of Secretary of State in respect of prisoners under sentence)—

(a) for "responsible medical officer" substitute "responsible clinician", and

(b) for "registered medical practitioner" substitute "approved clinician".

(3) In section 51 (further provisions as to detained persons)—

(a) in subsection (3)—

(i) for "responsible medical officer" substitute "responsible clinician", and

(ii) for "registered medical practitioner" substitute "approved clinician", and

(b) in subsection (4), for "responsible medical officer" substitute "responsible clinician".

(4) In section 52 (further provisions as to persons remanded by magistrates' courts), in subsections (5) and (7), for "responsible medical officer" substitute "responsible clinician".

(5) In section 53(2) (powers of Secretary of State in respect of civil prisoners and persons detained under the Immigration Acts)—

(a) for "responsible medical officer" substitute "responsible clinician", and

(b) for "registered medical practitioner" substitute "approved clinician".

(6) In section 54 (requirements as to medical evidence), for subsection (2) substitute—

"(2) For the purposes of any provision of this Part of this Act under which a court may act on the written evidence of any person, a report in writing purporting to be signed by that person may, subject to the provisions of this section, be received in evidence without proof of the following—

(a) the signature of the person; or

(b) his having the requisite qualifications or approval or authority or being of the requisite description to give the report.

(2A) But the court may require the signatory of any such report to be called to give oral evidence."

(7) In section 55 (interpretation of Part 3), for the definition of "responsible medical officer" in subsection (1) substitute—

"""responsible clinician", in relation to a person liable to be detained in a hospital within the meaning of Part 2 of this Act, means the approved clinician with overall responsibility for the patient's case."

(8) In Part 2 of Schedule 1 (modifications in relation to patients subject to special restrictions), in paragraph 3—

(a) in paragraph (b), for """the responsible medical officer" and after the words "that officer""" substitute """the responsible clinician" and after the words "that clinician""", and

(b) in paragraph (c), for """by the responsible medical officer""" substitute """by the responsible clinician""".

12 Amendments to Part 4 of 1983 Act

(1) Part 4 of the 1983 Act (consent to treatment) is amended as follows.

(2) In section 57 (requirements as to certification for treatment requiring consent and a second opinion)—

(a) in subsection (2)(a), for "responsible medical officer" substitute "responsible clinician (if there is one) or the person in charge of the treatment in question", and

(b) in subsection (3), for the words from ", and of those persons" to the end substitute "but, of those persons—

(a) one shall be a nurse and the other shall be neither a nurse nor a registered medical practitioner; and

(b) neither shall be the responsible clinician (if there is one) or the person in charge of the treatment in question."

(3) In section 58 (requirements as to certification for treatment requiring consent or a second opinion)—

(a) in subsection (3)—

(i) in paragraph (a), for "responsible medical officer" substitute "approved clinician in charge of it", and

(ii) in paragraph (b), for "responsible medical officer" substitute "responsible clinician or the approved clinician in charge of the treatment in question", and

(b) in subsection (4), for the words from ", and of those persons" to the end substitute "but, of those persons—

(a) one shall be a nurse and the other shall be neither a nurse nor a registered medical practitioner; and

(b) neither shall be the responsible clinician or the approved clinician in charge of the treatment in question."

(4) In section 61 (review of treatment)—

(a) in subsection (1)—

(i) for "by the responsible medical officer" substitute "by the approved clinician in charge of the treatment", and

(ii) in paragraph (a), for "responsible medical officer" substitute "responsible clinician",

(b) in subsection (2)(b), for "responsible medical officer" substitute "responsible clinician",

(c) in subsection (3), omit the words "to the responsible medical officer", and
(d) after that subsection insert—

"(3A) The notice under subsection (3) above shall be given to the approved clinician in charge of the treatment."

(5) In section 62(2) (exception to discontinuance of treatment), for "responsible medical officer" substitute "approved clinician in charge of the treatment".

(6) In section 63 (treatment not requiring consent), for "responsible medical officer" substitute "approved clinician in charge of the treatment".

(7) In section 64 (supplementary provisions for Part 4)—

(a) in subsection (1), for the words from ""the responsible" to "treatment" substitute ""the responsible clinician" means the approved clinician with overall responsibility for the case", and
(b) after that subsection insert—

"(1A) References in this Part of this Act to the approved clinician in charge of a patient's treatment shall, where the treatment in question is a form of treatment to which section 57 above applies, be construed as references to the person in charge of the treatment."

13 Amendments to Part 5 of 1983 Act

(1) Part 5 of the 1983 Act (Mental Health Review Tribunals) is amended as follows.

(2) In the following provisions, after "registered medical practitioner" insert "or approved clinician"—

(a) section 67(2) (power to visit and examine patient for the purposes of a tribunal reference), and
(b) section 76(1) (power to visit and examine patient for the purposes of a tribunal application).

(3) In section 79 (interpretation of Part 5), in subsection (6), for ", and "the responsible medical officer" means the responsible medical officer," substitute ", and "the responsible clinician" means the responsible clinician,".

14 Amendments to other provisions of 1983 Act

(1) The 1983 Act is amended as follows.

(2) In section 118 (code of practice), in subsection (1)(a), after "registered medical practitioners" insert ", approved clinicians".

(3) In the following provisions, after "registered medical practitioner" insert "or approved clinician"—

(a) section 120(4)(a) (right of person authorised by Secretary of State etc to visit patients), and
(b) section 121(5)(a) (right of person authorised by Mental Health Act Commission to visit patients).

(4) In section 134 (correspondence of patients), in subsection (1), for "registered medical practitioner in charge of the treatment of the patient" substitute "approved clinician with overall responsibility for the patient's case".

(5) In section 145 (general interpretation), in subsection (1), insert the following definition at the appropriate place—

> ""approved clinician" means a person approved by the Secretary of State (in relation to England) or by the Welsh Ministers (in relation to Wales) to act as an approved clinician for the purposes of this Act;".

15 Amendments to other Acts

(1) In section 116B(5) of the Army Act 1955 (3 & 4 Eliz. 2 c. 18) (provision for person subject to hospital order and restriction order to be remitted for trial, etc)—

- (a) for "the responsible medical officer" substitute "the responsible clinician", and
- (b) for the words from "In this subsection" to the end substitute—

> "In this subsection "responsible clinician" means the responsible clinician within the meaning of Part 3 of the 1983 Act."

(2) In section 116B(5) of the Air Force Act 1955 (3 & 4 Eliz. 2 c. 19) (provision for person subject to hospital order and restriction order to be remitted for trial, etc)—

- (a) for "the responsible medical officer" substitute "the responsible clinician", and
- (b) for the words from "In this subsection" to the end substitute—

> "In this subsection "responsible clinician" means the responsible clinician within the meaning of Part 3 of the 1983 Act."

(3) In section 63B(5) of the Naval Discipline Act 1957 (c. 53) (provision for person subject to hospital order and restriction order to be remitted for trial, etc)—

- (a) for "the responsible medical officer" substitute "the responsible clinician", and
- (b) for the words from "In this subsection" to the end substitute—

> "In this subsection "responsible clinician" means the responsible clinician within the meaning of Part 3 of the 1983 Act."

(4) In section 5A(4) of the Criminal Procedure (Insanity) Act 1964 (c. 84) (provision for person subject to hospital order and restriction order to be remitted for trial, etc), for "the responsible medical officer" substitute "the responsible clinician".

(5) In section 171 of the Armed Forces Act 2006 (c. 52) (remission for trial)—

- (a) in subsection (1), for "the responsible medical officer" substitute "the responsible clinician", and
- (b) in subsection (4) for the definition of "the responsible medical officer" substitute—

> ""the responsible clinician" means the responsible clinician within the meaning of Part 3 of the Mental Health Act 1983."

(6) On the commencement of the repeal of an enactment mentioned in subsection (1), (2) or (3) by the Armed Forces Act 2006, that subsection shall also cease to have effect.

16 Certain registered medical practitioners to be treated as approved under section 12 of 1983 Act

In section 12 of the 1983 Act (general provisions as to medical recommendations), after subsection (2) insert—

"(2A) A registered medical practitioner who is an approved clinician shall be treated as also approved for the purposes of this section under subsection (2) above as having special experience as mentioned there."

17 Regulations as to approvals in relation to England and Wales

After section 142 of the 1983 Act, insert—

"142A Regulations as to approvals in relation to England and Wales

The Secretary of State jointly with the Welsh Ministers may by regulations make provision as to the circumstances in which—

(a) a practitioner approved for the purposes of section 12 above, or

(b) a person approved to act as an approved clinician for the purposes of this Act,

approved in relation to England is to be treated, by virtue of his approval, as approved in relation to Wales too, and vice versa."

Approved mental health professionals

18 Approved mental health professionals

For section 114 of the 1983 Act (appointment of approved social workers) and the cross-heading immediately above it substitute—

"Approved mental health professionals

114 Approval by local social services authority

(1) A local social services authority may approve a person to act as an approved mental health professional for the purposes of this Act.

(2) But a local social services authority may not approve a registered medical practitioner to act as an approved mental health professional.

(3) Before approving a person under subsection (1) above, a local social services authority shall be satisfied that he has appropriate competence in dealing with persons who are suffering from mental disorder.

(4) The appropriate national authority may by regulations make provision in connection with the giving of approvals under subsection (1) above.

(5) The provision which may be made by regulations under subsection (4) above includes, in particular, provision as to—

(a) the period for which approvals under subsection (1) above have effect;

(b) the courses to be undertaken by persons before such approvals are to be given and during the period for which such approvals have effect;

(c) the conditions subject to which such approvals are to be given; and

(d) the factors to be taken into account in determining whether persons have appropriate competence as mentioned in subsection (3) above.

(6) Provision made by virtue of subsection (5)(b) above may relate to courses approved or provided by such person as may be specified in the regulations (as well as to courses approved under section 114A below).

(7) An approval by virtue of subsection (6) above may be in respect of a course in general or in respect of a course in relation to a particular person.

(8) The power to make regulations under subsection (4) above includes power to make different provision for different cases or areas.

(9) In this section "the appropriate national authority" means—

(a) in relation to persons who are or wish to become approved to act as approved mental health professionals by a local social services authority whose area is in England, the Secretary of State;

(b) in relation to persons who are or wish to become approved to act as approved mental health professionals by a local social services authority whose area is in Wales, the Welsh Ministers.

(10) In this Act "approved mental health professional" means—

(a) in relation to acting on behalf of a local social services authority whose area is in England, a person approved under subsection (1) above by any local social services authority whose area is in England, and

(b) in relation to acting on behalf of a local social services authority whose area is in Wales, a person approved under that subsection by any local social services authority whose area is in Wales."

19 Approval of courses etc for approved mental health professionals

After section 114 of the 1983 Act insert—

"114A Approval of courses etc for approved mental health professionals

(1) The relevant Council may, in accordance with rules made by it, approve courses for persons who are or wish to become approved mental health professionals.

(2) For that purpose—

(a) subsections (2) to (4)(a) and (7) of section 63 of the Care Standards Act 2000 apply as they apply to approvals given, rules made and courses approved under that section; and

(b) sections 66 and 71 of that Act apply accordingly.

(3) In subsection (1), "the relevant Council" means—

(a) in relation to persons who are or wish to become approved to act as approved mental health professionals by a local social services authority whose area is in England, the General Social Care Council;

(b) in relation to persons who are or wish to become approved to act as approved mental health professionals by a local social services authority whose area is in Wales, the Care Council for Wales.

(4) The functions of an approved mental health professional shall not be considered to be relevant social work for the purposes of Part 4 of the Care Standards Act 2000.

(5) The General Social Care Council and the Care Council for Wales may also carry out, or assist other persons in carrying out, research into matters relevant to training for approved mental health professionals."

20 Amendment to section 62 of Care Standards Act 2000

In section 62 of the Care Standards Act 2000 (c. 14) (codes of practice), after subsection (1) insert—

"(1A) The codes may also lay down standards of conduct and practice expected of social workers when carrying out the functions of an approved mental health professional (as defined in section 114 of the Mental Health Act 1983)."

21 Approved mental health professionals: further amendments

Schedule 2 (which contains amendments in connection with section 18) has effect.

Conflicts of interest in professional roles

22 Conflicts of interest

(1) The 1983 Act is amended as follows.

(2) In section 11 (general provisions as to applications), after subsection (1) insert—

"(1A) No application mentioned in subsection (1) above shall be made by an approved mental health professional if the circumstances are such that there would be a potential conflict of interest for the purposes of regulations under section 12A below."

(3) In section 12 (general provisions as to medical recommendations), in subsection (1), after "this Part of this Act" insert "or a guardianship application".

(4) In that section, for subsections (3) to (7) substitute—

"(3) No medical recommendation shall be given for the purposes of an application mentioned in subsection (1) above if the circumstances are such that there would be a potential conflict of interest for the purposes of regulations under section 12A below."

(5) After that section insert—

"12A Conflicts of interest

(1) The appropriate national authority may make regulations as to the circumstances in which there would be a potential conflict of interest such that—

(a) an approved mental health professional shall not make an application mentioned in section 11(1) above;

(b) a registered medical practitioner shall not give a recommendation for the purposes of an application mentioned in section 12(1) above.

(2) Regulations under subsection (1) above may make—

(a) provision for the prohibitions in paragraphs (a) and (b) of that subsection to be subject to specified exceptions;

(b) different provision for different cases; and

(c) transitional, consequential, incidental or supplemental provision.

(3) In subsection (1) above, "the appropriate national authority" means—

(a) in relation to applications in which admission is sought to a hospital in England or to guardianship applications in respect of which the area of the relevant local social services authority is in England, the Secretary of State;

(b) in relation to applications in which admission is sought to a hospital in Wales or to guardianship applications in respect of which the area of the relevant local social services authority is in Wales, the Welsh Ministers.

(4) References in this section to the relevant local social services authority, in relation to a guardianship application, are references to the local social services authority named in the application as guardian or (as the case may be) the local social services authority for the area in which the person so named resides."

(6) In section 13 (duty to make applications for admission or guardianship), in subsection (5), after "section 11(4) above" insert "or of regulations under section 12A above".

CHAPTER 3

SAFEGUARDS FOR PATIENTS

Patient's nearest relative

23 Extension of power to appoint acting nearest relative

(1) Section 29 of the 1983 Act (appointment by court of acting nearest relative) is amended as follows.

(2) In subsection (1), for the words from "the applicant" to the end substitute "the person specified in the order".

(3) After subsection (1) insert—

"(1A) If the court decides to make an order on an application under subsection (1) above, the following rules have effect for the purposes of specifying a person in the order—

(a) if a person is nominated in the application to act as the patient's nearest relative and that person is, in the opinion of the court, a suitable person to act as such and is willing to do so, the court shall specify that person (or, if there are two or more such persons, such one of them as the court thinks fit);

(b) otherwise, the court shall specify such person as is, in its opinion, a suitable person to act as the patient's nearest relative and is willing to do so."

(4) In subsection (2)—

(a) after "on the application of—" insert—

"(za) the patient;", and

(b) omit the words from "but in relation to" to the end.

(5) In subsection (3)—

(a) in paragraph (c) omit the word "or" at the end of the paragraph, and

(b) after paragraph (d) insert "; or

(e) that the nearest relative of the patient is otherwise not a suitable person to act as such."

(6) In subsection (5), for "(3)(a) or (b)" substitute "(3)(a), (b) or (e)".

24 Discharge and variation of orders appointing nearest relative

(1) Section 30 of the 1983 Act (discharge and variation of orders under section 29) is amended as follows.

(2) In subsection (1)—

(a) in paragraph (a), after "in any case, by" insert "the patient or", and

(b) in paragraph (b), for "or paragraph (b)" substitute ", (b) or (e)".

(3) After that subsection insert—

"(1A) But, in the case of an order made on the ground specified in paragraph (e) of section 29(3) above, an application may not be made under subsection (1)(b) above by the person who was the nearest relative of the patient when the order was made except with leave of the county court."

(4) In subsection (2)—

(a) after "or on the application of" insert "the patient or of", and

(b) for the words from "for the first-mentioned person" to the end substitute "another person for the person having those functions".

(5) After that subsection insert—

"(2A) If the court decides to vary an order on an application under subsection (2) above, the following rules have effect for the purposes of substituting another person—

(a) if a person is nominated in the application to act as the patient's nearest relative and that person is, in the opinion of the court, a suitable person to act as such and is willing to do so, the court shall specify that person (or, if there are two or more such persons, such one of them as the court thinks fit);

(b) otherwise, the court shall specify such person as is, in its opinion, a suitable person to act as the patient's nearest relative and is willing to do so."

(6) In subsection (4), for the words from "An order under" to "period is specified" substitute "An order made on the ground specified in paragraph (c) or (d) of section 29(3) above shall, unless previously discharged under subsection (1) above, cease to have effect as follows".

(7) After subsection (4A) (inserted by Schedule 3 to this Act) insert—

"(4B) An order made on the ground specified in paragraph (a), (b) or (e) of section 29(3) above shall—

(a) if a period was specified under section 29(5) above, cease to have effect on expiry of that period, unless previously discharged under subsection (1) above;

(b) if no such period was specified, remain in force until it is discharged under subsection (1) above."

25 Restriction of nearest relative's right to apply to tribunal

In section 66 of the 1983 Act (applications to tribunal), in subsection (1)(h) after "section 29 above" insert "on the ground specified in paragraph (c) or (d) of subsection (3) of that section".

26 Civil partners

(1) Section 26 of the 1983 Act (definition of "relative" and "nearest relative") is amended as set out in subsections (2) to (5).

(2) In subsection (1)(a), after "wife" insert "or civil partner".

(3) In subsection (5)—

(a) in paragraph (b) after "wife" insert "or civil partner", and

(b) in paragraph (c) after "wife," insert "civil partner,".

(4) In subsection (6)—

(a) for "and "wife" include a person who is living with the patient as the patient's husband or wife" substitute ", "wife" and "civil partner" include a person who is living with the patient as the patient's husband or wife or as if they were civil partners", and

(b) for "unless the husband or wife" substitute "or a patient in a civil partnership unless the husband, wife or civil partner".

(5) In subsection (7)(b), for "unless the husband or wife" substitute "or a patient in a civil partnership unless the husband, wife or civil partner".

(6) In section 27 of the 1983 Act (children and young persons in care), after "wife" insert "or civil partner".

Consent to treatment

27 Electro-convulsive therapy, etc.

After section 58 of the 1983 Act insert—

"58A Electro-convulsive therapy, etc.

(1) This section applies to the following forms of medical treatment for mental disorder—

(a) electro-convulsive therapy; and

(b) such other forms of treatment as may be specified for the purposes of this section by regulations made by the appropriate national authority.

(2) Subject to section 62 below, a patient shall be not be given any form of treatment to which this section applies unless he falls within subsection (3), (4) or (5) below.

(3) A patient falls within this subsection if—

(a) he has attained the age of 18 years;

(b) he has consented to the treatment in question; and

(c) either the approved clinician in charge of it or a registered medical practitioner appointed as mentioned in section 58(3) above has certified in writing that the patient is capable of understanding the nature, purpose and likely effects of the treatment and has consented to it.

(4) A patient falls within this subsection if—

(a) he has not attained the age of 18 years; but

(b) he has consented to the treatment in question; and

(c) a registered medical practitioner appointed as aforesaid (not being the approved clinician in charge of the treatment) has certified in writing—

(i) that the patient is capable of understanding the nature, purpose and likely effects of the treatment and has consented to it; and

(ii) that it is appropriate for the treatment to be given.

(5) A patient falls within this subsection if a registered medical practitioner appointed as aforesaid (not being the responsible clinician (if there is one) or the approved clinician in charge of the treatment in question) has certified in writing—

(a) that the patient is not capable of understanding the nature, purpose and likely effects of the treatment; but

(b) that it is appropriate for the treatment to be given; and

(c) that giving him the treatment would not conflict with—

(i) an advance decision which the registered medical practitioner concerned is satisfied is valid and applicable; or

(ii) a decision made by a donee or deputy or by the Court of Protection.

(6) Before giving a certificate under subsection (5) above the registered medical practitioner concerned shall consult two other persons who have been professionally concerned with the patient's medical treatment but, of those persons—

(a) one shall be a nurse and the other shall be neither a nurse nor a registered medical practitioner; and

(b) neither shall be the responsible clinician (if there is one) or the approved clinician in charge of the treatment in question.

(7) This section shall not by itself confer sufficient authority for a patient who falls within section 56(5) above to be given a form of treatment to which this section applies if he is not capable of understanding the nature, purpose and likely effects of the treatment (and cannot therefore consent to it).

(8) Before making any regulations for the purposes of this section, the appropriate national authority shall consult such bodies as appear to it to be concerned.

(9) In this section—

(a) a reference to an advance decision is to an advance decision (within the meaning of the Mental Capacity Act 2005) made by the patient;

(b) "valid and applicable", in relation to such a decision, means valid and applicable to the treatment in question in accordance with section 25 of that Act;

(c) a reference to a donee is to a donee of a lasting power of attorney (within the meaning of section 9 of that Act) created by the patient, where the donee is acting within the scope of his authority and in accordance with that Act; and

(d) a reference to a deputy is to a deputy appointed for the patient by the Court of Protection under section 16 of that Act, where the deputy is acting within the scope of his authority and in accordance with that Act.

(10) In this section, "the appropriate national authority" means—

(a) in a case where the treatment in question would, if given, be given in England, the Secretary of State;

(b) in a case where the treatment in question would, if given, be given in Wales, the Welsh Ministers."

28 Section 27: supplemental

(1) Part 4 of the 1983 Act (consent to treatment) is amended as follows.

(2) In section 58 (treatment requiring consent or a second opinion)—

(a) in subsection (1)(b), after "section 57 above" insert "or section 58A(1)(b) below", and

(b) in subsection (3)(b), before "has not consented to it" insert "being so capable".

(3) In section 59 (plans of treatment), for "or 58" substitute ", 58 or 58A".

(4) In section 60 (withdrawal of consent), for "or 58", substitute ", 58 or 58A".

(5) In section 61 (review of treatment)—

(a) in subsection (1), for "or 58(3)(b)" substitute ", 58(3)(b) or 58A(4) or (5)", and

(b) in subsection (3)—

(i) for "or 58(3)(b)" substitute ", 58(3)(b) or 58A(4) or (5)", and

(ii) for "and 58" substitute ", 58 and 58A".

(6) In section 62 (urgent treatment), after subsection (1) insert—

"(1A) Section 58A above, in so far as it relates to electro-convulsive therapy by virtue of subsection (1)(a) of that section, shall not apply to any treatment which falls within paragraph (a) or (b) of subsection (1) above.

(1B) Section 58A above, in so far as it relates to a form of treatment specified by virtue of subsection (1)(b) of that section, shall not apply to any treatment which falls within such of paragraphs (a) to (d) of subsection (1) above as may be specified in regulations under that section.

(1C) For the purposes of subsection (1B) above, the regulations—

(a) may make different provision for different cases (and may, in particular, make different provision for different forms of treatment);

(b) may make provision which applies subject to specified exceptions; and

(c) may include transitional, consequential, incidental or supplemental provision."

(7) In that section, in subsection (2), for "or 58" substitute ", 58 or 58A".

(8) In section 63 (treatment not requiring consent), for ", not being treatment falling within section 57 or 58 above," substitute ", not being a form of treatment to which section 57, 58 or 58A above applies,".

(9) In section 64 (supplementary provisions), after subsection (1A) (inserted by section 12 of this Act) insert—

"(1B) References in this Part of this Act to the approved clinician in charge of a patient's treatment shall, where the treatment in question is a form of treatment to which section 58A above applies and the patient falls within section 56(5) above, be construed as references to the person in charge of the treatment.

(1C) Regulations made by virtue of section 32(2)(d) above apply for the purposes of this Part as they apply for the purposes of Part 2 of this Act."

(10) In section 28 of the Mental Capacity Act 2005 (c. 9) (Mental Health Act matters), after subsection (1) insert—

"(1A) Subsection (1) does not apply in relation to any form of treatment to which section 58A of that Act (electro-convulsive therapy, etc.) applies if the patient comes within subsection (7) of that section (informal patient under 18 who cannot give consent).".

29 Withdrawal of consent

(1) Section 60 of the 1983 Act (withdrawal of consent) is amended as follows.

(2) After subsection (1) insert—

"(1A) Subsection (1B) below applies where—

(a) the consent of a patient to any treatment has been given for the purposes of section 57, 58 or 58A above; but

(b) before the completion of the treatment, the patient ceases to be capable of understanding its nature, purpose and likely effects.

(1B) The patient shall, subject to section 62 below, be treated as having withdrawn his consent, and those sections shall then apply as if the remainder of the treatment were a separate form of treatment.

(1C) Subsection (1D) below applies where—

(a) a certificate has been given under section 58 or 58A above that a patient is not capable of understanding the nature, purpose and likely effects of the treatment to which the certificate applies; but

(b) before the completion of the treatment, the patient becomes capable of understanding its nature, purpose and likely effects.

(1D) The certificate shall, subject to section 62 below, cease to apply to the treatment and those sections shall then apply as if the remainder of the treatment were a separate form of treatment."

(3) In subsection (2), for "subsection (1)" substitute "subsections (1) to (1D)".

Advocacy

30 Independent mental health advocates

(1) Part 10 of the 1983 Act (miscellaneous and supplementary) is amended as follows.

(2) Before section 131 insert—

"130A Independent mental health advocates

(1) The appropriate national authority shall make such arrangements as it considers reasonable to enable persons ("independent mental health advocates") to be available to help qualifying patients.

(2) The appropriate national authority may by regulations make provision as to the appointment of persons as independent mental health advocates.

(3) The regulations may, in particular, provide—

(a) that a person may act as an independent mental health advocate only in such circumstances, or only subject to such conditions, as may be specified in the regulations;

(b) for the appointment of a person as an independent mental health advocate to be subject to approval in accordance with the regulations.

(4) In making arrangements under this section, the appropriate national authority shall have regard to the principle that any help available to a patient under the arrangements should, so far as practicable, be provided by a person who is independent of any person who is professionally concerned with the patient's medical treatment.

(5) For the purposes of subsection (4) above, a person is not to be regarded as professionally concerned with a patient's medical treatment merely because he is representing him in accordance with arrangements—

(a) under section 35 of the Mental Capacity Act 2005; or

(b) of a description specified in regulations under this section.

(6) Arrangements under this section may include provision for payments to be made to, or in relation to, persons carrying out functions in accordance with the arrangements.

(7) Regulations under this section—

(a) may make different provision for different cases;

(b) may make provision which applies subject to specified exceptions;

(c) may include transitional, consequential, incidental or supplemental provision.

130B Arrangements under section 130A

(1) The help available to a qualifying patient under arrangements under section 130A above shall include help in obtaining information about and understanding—

(a) the provisions of this Act by virtue of which he is a qualifying patient;

(b) any conditions or restrictions to which he is subject by virtue of this Act;

(c) what (if any) medical treatment is given to him or is proposed or discussed in his case;

(d) why it is given, proposed or discussed;

(e) the authority under which it is, or would be, given; and

(f) the requirements of this Act which apply, or would apply, in connection with the giving of the treatment to him.

(2) The help available under the arrangements to a qualifying patient shall also include—

(a) help in obtaining information about and understanding any rights which may be exercised under this Act by or in relation to him; and

(b) help (by way of representation or otherwise) in exercising those rights.

(3) For the purpose of providing help to a patient in accordance with the arrangements, an independent mental health advocate may—

(a) visit and interview the patient in private;

(b) visit and interview any person who is professionally concerned with his medical treatment;

(c) require the production of and inspect any records relating to his detention or treatment in any hospital or registered establishment or to any after-care services provided for him under section 117 above;

(d) require the production of and inspect any records of, or held by, a local social services authority which relate to him.

(4) But an independent mental health advocate is not entitled to the production of, or to inspect, records in reliance on subsection (3)(c) or (d) above unless—

(a) in a case where the patient has capacity or is competent to consent, he does consent; or

(b) in any other case, the production or inspection would not conflict with a decision made by a donee or deputy or the Court of Protection and the person holding the records, having regard to such matters as may be prescribed in regulations under section 130A above, considers that—

(i) the records may be relevant to the help to be provided by the advocate; and

(ii) the production or inspection is appropriate.

(5) For the purpose of providing help to a patient in accordance with the arrangements, an independent mental health advocate shall comply with any reasonable request made to him by any of the following for him to visit and interview the patient—

(a) the person (if any) appearing to the advocate to be the patient's nearest relative;

(b) the responsible clinician for the purposes of this Act;

(c) an approved mental health professional.

(6) But nothing in this Act prevents the patient from declining to be provided with help under the arrangements.

(7) In subsection (4) above—

(a) the reference to a patient who has capacity is to be read in accordance with the Mental Capacity Act 2005;

(b) the reference to a donee is to a donee of a lasting power of attorney (within the meaning of section 9 of that Act) created by the patient, where the donee is acting within the scope of his authority and in accordance with that Act;

(c) the reference to a deputy is to a deputy appointed for the patient by the Court of Protection under section 16 of that Act, where the deputy is acting within the scope of his authority and in accordance with that Act.

130C Section 130A: supplemental

(1) This section applies for the purposes of section 130A above.

(2) A patient is a qualifying patient if he is—

(a) liable to be detained under this Act (otherwise than by virtue of section 4 or 5(2) or (4) above or section 135 or 136 below);

(b) subject to guardianship under this Act; or

(c) a community patient.

(3) A patient is also a qualifying patient if—

(a) not being a qualifying patient falling within subsection (2) above, he discusses with a registered medical practitioner or approved clinician the possibility of being given a form of treatment to which section 57 above applies; or

(b) not having attained the age of 18 years and not being a qualifying patient falling within subsection (2) above, he discusses with a registered medical practitioner or approved clinician the possibility of being given a form of treatment to which section 58A above applies.

(4) Where a patient who is a qualifying patient falling within subsection (3) above is informed that the treatment concerned is proposed in his case, he remains a qualifying patient falling within that subsection until—

(a) the proposal is withdrawn; or

(b) the treatment is completed or discontinued.

(5) References to the appropriate national authority are—

(a) in relation to a qualifying patient in England, to the Secretary of State;

(b) in relation to a qualifying patient in Wales, to the Welsh Ministers.

(6) For the purposes of subsection (5) above—

(a) a qualifying patient falling within subsection (2)(a) above is to be regarded as being in the territory in which the hospital or registered establishment in which he is liable to be detained is situated;

(b) a qualifying patient falling within subsection (2)(b) above is to be regarded as being in the territory in which the area of the responsible local social services authority within the meaning of section 34(3) above is situated;

(c) a qualifying patient falling within subsection (2)(c) above is to be regarded as being in the territory in which the responsible hospital is situated;

(d) a qualifying patient falling within subsection (3) above is to be regarded as being in the territory determined in accordance with arrangements made for the purposes of this paragraph, and published, by the Secretary of State and the Welsh Ministers.

130D Duty to give information about independent mental health advocates

(1) The responsible person in relation to a qualifying patient (within the meaning given by section 130C above) shall take such steps as are practicable to ensure that the patient understands—

(a) that help is available to him from an independent mental health advocate; and

(b) how he can obtain that help.

(2) In subsection (1) above, "the responsible person" means—

(a) in relation to a qualifying patient falling within section 130C(2)(a) above (other than one also falling within paragraph (b) below), the managers of the hospital or registered establishment in which he is liable to be detained;

(b) in relation to a qualifying patient falling within section 130C(2)(a) above and conditionally discharged by virtue of section 42(2), 73 or 74 above, the responsible clinician;

(c) in relation to a qualifying patient falling within section 130C(2)(b) above, the responsible local social services authority within the meaning of section 34(3) above;

(d) in relation to a qualifying patient falling within section 130C(2)(c) above, the managers of the responsible hospital;

(e) in relation to a qualifying patient falling within section 130C(3) above, the registered medical practitioner or approved clinician with whom the patient first discusses the possibility of being given the treatment concerned.

(3) The steps to be taken under subsection (1) above shall be taken—

(a) where the responsible person falls within subsection (2)(a) above, as soon as practicable after the patient becomes liable to be detained;

(b) where the responsible person falls within subsection (2)(b) above, as soon as practicable after the conditional discharge;

(c) where the responsible person falls within subsection (2)(c) above, as soon as practicable after the patient becomes subject to guardianship;

(d) where the responsible person falls within subsection (2)(d) above, as soon as practicable after the patient becomes a community patient;

(e) where the responsible person falls within subsection (2)(e) above, while the discussion with the patient is taking place or as soon as practicable thereafter.

(4) The steps to be taken under subsection (1) above shall include giving the requisite information both orally and in writing.

(5) The responsible person in relation to a qualifying patient falling within section 130C(2) above (other than a patient liable to be detained by virtue of Part 3 of this Act) shall, except where the patient otherwise requests, take such steps as are practicable to furnish the person (if any) appearing to the responsible person to be the patient's nearest relative with a copy of any information given to the patient in writing under subsection (1) above.

(6) The steps to be taken under subsection (5) above shall be taken when the information concerned is given to the patient or within a reasonable time thereafter."

(3) In section 134 (patients' correspondence), in subsection (3A), for paragraph (b) substitute—

"(b) "independent advocacy services" means services provided under—

(i) arrangements under section 130A above;

(ii) arrangements under section 248 of the National Health Service Act 2006 or section 187 of the National Health Service (Wales) Act 2006; or

(iii) arrangements of a description prescribed as mentioned in paragraph (a) above."

Accommodation, etc.

31 Accommodation, etc.

(1) The 1983 Act is amended as follows.

(2) In section 39 (power of court to request information about hospitals), after subsection (1) insert—

"(1A) In relation to a person who has not attained the age of 18 years, subsection (1) above shall have effect as if the reference to the making of a hospital order included a reference to a remand under section 35 or 36 above or the making of an order under section 44 below.

(1B) Where the person concerned has not attained the age of 18 years, the information which may be requested under subsection (1) above includes, in particular, information about the availability of accommodation or facilities designed so as to be specially suitable for patients who have not attained the age of 18 years."

(3) After section 131 insert—

"131A Accommodation, etc. for children

(1) This section applies in respect of any patient who has not attained the age of 18 years and who—

(a) is liable to be detained in a hospital under this Act; or

(b) is admitted to, or remains in, a hospital in pursuance of such arrangements as are mentioned in section 131(1) above.

(2) The managers of the hospital shall ensure that the patient's environment in the hospital is suitable having regard to his age (subject to his needs).

(3) For the purpose of deciding how to fulfil the duty under subsection (2) above, the managers shall consult a person who appears to them to have knowledge or experience of cases involving patients who have not attained the age of 18 years which makes him suitable to be consulted.

(4) In this section, "hospital" includes a registered establishment."

(4) In section 140 (the title to which becomes "Notification of hospitals having arrangements for special cases"), for the words from "for the reception" to the end substitute "—

(a) for the reception of patients in cases of special urgency;

(b) for the provision of accommodation or facilities designed so as to be specially suitable for patients who have not attained the age of 18 years."

CHAPTER 4

SUPERVISED COMMUNITY TREATMENT

32 Community treatment orders, etc

(1) The 1983 Act is amended as follows.

(2) After section 17 insert—

"17A Community treatment orders

(1) The responsible clinician may by order in writing discharge a detained patient from hospital subject to his being liable to recall in accordance with section 17E below.

(2) A detained patient is a patient who is liable to be detained in a hospital in pursuance of an application for admission for treatment.

(3) An order under subsection (1) above is referred to in this Act as a "community treatment order".

(4) The responsible clinician may not make a community treatment order unless—

- (a) in his opinion, the relevant criteria are met; and
- (b) an approved mental health professional states in writing—
  - (i) that he agrees with that opinion; and
  - (ii) that it is appropriate to make the order.

(5) The relevant criteria are—

- (a) the patient is suffering from mental disorder of a nature or degree which makes it appropriate for him to receive medical treatment;
- (b) it is necessary for his health or safety or for the protection of other persons that he should receive such treatment;
- (c) subject to his being liable to be recalled as mentioned in paragraph (d) below, such treatment can be provided without his continuing to be detained in a hospital;
- (d) it is necessary that the responsible clinician should be able to exercise the power under section 17E(1) below to recall the patient to hospital; and
- (e) appropriate medical treatment is available for him.

(6) In determining whether the criterion in subsection (5)(d) above is met, the responsible clinician shall, in particular, consider, having regard to the patient's history of mental disorder and any other relevant factors, what risk there would be of a deterioration of the patient's condition if he were not detained in a hospital (as a result, for example, of his refusing or neglecting to receive the medical treatment he requires for his mental disorder).

(7) In this Act—

"community patient" means a patient in respect of whom a community treatment order is in force;

"the community treatment order", in relation to such a patient, means the community treatment order in force in respect of him; and

"the responsible hospital", in relation to such a patient, means the hospital in which he was liable to be detained immediately before the community treatment order was made, subject to section 19A below.

17B Conditions

(1) A community treatment order shall specify conditions to which the patient is to be subject while the order remains in force.

(2) But, subject to subsection (3) below, the order may specify conditions only if the responsible clinician, with the agreement of the approved mental health professional mentioned in section 17A(4)(b) above, thinks them necessary or appropriate for one or more of the following purposes—

- (a) ensuring that the patient receives medical treatment;

(b) preventing risk of harm to the patient's health or safety;

(c) protecting other persons.

(3) The order shall specify—

(a) a condition that the patient make himself available for examination under section 20A below; and

(b) a condition that, if it is proposed to give a certificate under Part 4A of this Act in his case, he make himself available for examination so as to enable the certificate to be given.

(4) The responsible clinician may from time to time by order in writing vary the conditions specified in a community treatment order.

(5) He may also suspend any conditions specified in a community treatment order.

(6) If a community patient fails to comply with a condition specified in the community treatment order by virtue of subsection (2) above, that fact may be taken into account for the purposes of exercising the power of recall under section 17E(1) below.

(7) But nothing in this section restricts the exercise of that power to cases where there is such a failure.

17C Duration of community treatment order

A community treatment order shall remain in force until—

(a) the period mentioned in section 20A(1) below (as extended under any provision of this Act) expires, but this is subject to sections 21 and 22 below;

(b) the patient is discharged in pursuance of an order under section 23 below or a direction under section 72 below;

(c) the application for admission for treatment in respect of the patient otherwise ceases to have effect; or

(d) the order is revoked under section 17F below,

whichever occurs first.

17D Effect of community treatment order

(1) The application for admission for treatment in respect of a patient shall not cease to have effect by virtue of his becoming a community patient.

(2) But while he remains a community patient—

(a) the authority of the managers to detain him under section 6(2) above in pursuance of that application shall be suspended; and

(b) reference (however expressed) in this or any other Act, or in any subordinate legislation (within the meaning of the Interpretation Act 1978), to patients liable to be detained, or detained, under this Act shall not include him.

(3) And section 20 below shall not apply to him while he remains a community patient.

(4) Accordingly, authority for his detention shall not expire during any period in which that authority is suspended by virtue of subsection (2)(a) above.

17E Power to recall to hospital

(1) The responsible clinician may recall a community patient to hospital if in his opinion—

(a) the patient requires medical treatment in hospital for his mental disorder; and

(b) there would be a risk of harm to the health or safety of the patient or to other persons if the patient were not recalled to hospital for that purpose.

(2) The responsible clinician may also recall a community patient to hospital if the patient fails to comply with a condition specified under section 17B(3) above.

(3) The hospital to which a patient is recalled need not be the responsible hospital.

(4) Nothing in this section prevents a patient from being recalled to a hospital even though he is already in the hospital at the time when the power of recall is exercised; references to recalling him shall be construed accordingly.

(5) The power of recall under subsections (1) and (2) above shall be exercisable by notice in writing to the patient.

(6) A notice under this section recalling a patient to hospital shall be sufficient authority for the managers of that hospital to detain the patient there in accordance with the provisions of this Act.

17F Powers in respect of recalled patients

(1) This section applies to a community patient who is detained in a hospital by virtue of a notice recalling him there under section 17E above.

(2) The patient may be transferred to another hospital in such circumstances and subject to such conditions as may be prescribed in regulations made by the Secretary of State (if the hospital in which the patient is detained is in England) or the Welsh Ministers (if that hospital is in Wales).

(3) If he is so transferred to another hospital, he shall be treated for the purposes of this section (and section 17E above) as if the notice under that section were a notice recalling him to that other hospital and as if he had been detained there from the time when his detention in hospital by virtue of the notice first began.

(4) The responsible clinician may by order in writing revoke the community treatment order if—

(a) in his opinion, the conditions mentioned in section 3(2) above are satisfied in respect of the patient; and

(b) an approved mental health professional states in writing—

(i) that he agrees with that opinion; and

(ii) that it is appropriate to revoke the order.

(5) The responsible clinician may at any time release the patient under this section, but not after the community treatment order has been revoked.

(6) If the patient has not been released, nor the community treatment order revoked, by the end of the period of 72 hours, he shall then be released.

(7) But a patient who is released under this section remains subject to the community treatment order.

(8) In this section—

(a) "the period of 72 hours" means the period of 72 hours beginning with the time when the patient's detention in hospital by virtue of the notice under section 17E above begins; and

(b) references to being released shall be construed as references to being released from that detention (and accordingly from being recalled to hospital).

17G Effect of revoking community treatment order

(1) This section applies if a community treatment order is revoked under section 17F above in respect of a patient.

(2) Section 6(2) above shall have effect as if the patient had never been discharged from hospital by virtue of the community treatment order.

(3) The provisions of this or any other Act relating to patients liable to be detained (or detained) in pursuance of an application for admission for treatment shall apply to the patient as they did before the community treatment order was made, unless otherwise provided.

(4) If, when the order is revoked, the patient is being detained in a hospital other than the responsible hospital, the provisions of this Part of this Act shall have effect as if—

(a) the application for admission for treatment in respect of him were an application for admission to that other hospital; and

(b) he had been admitted to that other hospital at the time when he was originally admitted in pursuance of the application.

(5) But, in any case, section 20 below shall have effect as if the patient had been admitted to hospital in pursuance of the application for admission for treatment on the day on which the order is revoked."

(3) After section 20 (the cross-heading immediately above which becomes "Duration of authority and discharge") insert—

"20A Community treatment period

(1) Subject to the provisions of this Part of this Act, a community treatment order shall cease to be in force on expiry of the period of six months beginning with the day on which it was made.

(2) That period is referred to in this Act as "the community treatment period".

(3) The community treatment period may, unless the order has previously ceased to be in force, be extended—

(a) from its expiration for a period of six months;

(b) from the expiration of any period of extension under paragraph (a) above for a further period of one year,

and so on for periods of one year at a time.

(4) Within the period of two months ending on the day on which the order would cease to be in force in default of an extension under this section, it shall be the duty of the responsible clinician—

(a) to examine the patient; and

(b) if it appears to him that the conditions set out in subsection (6) below are satisfied and if a statement under subsection (8) below is made, to furnish to the managers of the responsible hospital a report to that effect in the prescribed form.

(5) Where such a report is furnished in respect of the patient, the managers shall, unless they discharge him under section 23 below, cause him to be informed.

(6) The conditions referred to in subsection (4) above are that—

(a) the patient is suffering from mental disorder of a nature or degree which makes it appropriate for him to receive medical treatment;

(b) it is necessary for his health or safety or for the protection of other persons that he should receive such treatment;

(c) subject to his continuing to be liable to be recalled as mentioned in paragraph (d) below, such treatment can be provided without his being detained in a hospital;

(d) it is necessary that the responsible clinician should continue to be able to exercise the power under section 17E(1) above to recall the patient to hospital; and

(e) appropriate medical treatment is available for him.

(7) In determining whether the criterion in subsection (6)(d) above is met, the responsible clinician shall, in particular, consider, having regard to the patient's history of mental disorder and any other relevant factors, what risk there would be of a deterioration of the patient's condition if he were to continue not to be detained in a hospital (as a result, for example, of his refusing or neglecting to receive the medical treatment he requires for his mental disorder).

(8) The statement referred to in subsection (4) above is a statement in writing by an approved mental health professional—

(a) that it appears to him that the conditions set out in subsection (6) above are satisfied; and

(b) that it is appropriate to extend the community treatment period.

(9) Before furnishing a report under subsection (4) above the responsible clinician shall consult one or more other persons who have been professionally concerned with the patient's medical treatment.

(10) Where a report is duly furnished under subsection (4) above, the community treatment period shall be thereby extended for the period prescribed in that case by subsection (3) above.

20B Effect of expiry of community treatment order

(1) A community patient shall be deemed to be discharged absolutely from liability to recall under this Part of this Act, and the application for admission for treatment cease to have effect, on expiry of the community treatment order, if the order has not previously ceased to be in force.

(2) For the purposes of subsection (1) above, a community treatment order expires on expiry of the community treatment period as extended under this Part of this Act, but this is subject to sections 21 and 22 below."

(4) Schedules 3 and 4 (which contain further amendments) have effect.

33 Relationship with leave of absence

(1) The 1983 Act is amended as follows.

(2) In section 17 (leave of absence from hospital), after subsection (2) insert—

"(2A) But longer-term leave may not be granted to a patient unless the responsible clinician first considers whether the patient should be dealt with under section 17A instead.

(2B) For these purposes, longer-term leave is granted to a patient if—

(a) leave of absence is granted to him under this section either indefinitely or for a specified period of more than seven consecutive days; or

(b) a specified period is extended under this section such that the total period for which leave of absence will have been granted to him under this section exceeds seven consecutive days."

(3) In Part 2 of Schedule 1 (patients subject to special restrictions), in paragraph 3 after paragraph (a) insert—

"(aa) subsections (2A) and (2B) shall be omitted;".

34 Consent to treatment

(1) Part 4 of the 1983 Act (consent to treatment) is amended as follows.

(2) For section 56 substitute—

"56 Patients to whom Part 4 applies

(1) Section 57 and, so far as relevant to that section, sections 59 to 62 below apply to any patient.

(2) Subject to that and to subsection (5) below, this Part of this Act applies to a patient only if he falls within subsection (3) or (4) below.

(3) A patient falls within this subsection if he is liable to be detained under this Act but not if—

(a) he is so liable by virtue of an emergency application and the second medical recommendation referred to in section 4(4)(a) above has not been given and received;

(b) he is so liable by virtue of section 5(2) or (4) or 35 above or section 135 or 136 below or by virtue of a direction for his detention in a place of safety under section 37(4) or 45A(5) above; or

(c) he has been conditionally discharged under section 42(2) above or section 73 or 74 below and he is not recalled to hospital.

(4) A patient falls within this subsection if—

(a) he is a community patient; and

(b) he is recalled to hospital under section 17E above.

(5) Section 58A and, so far as relevant to that section, sections 59 to 62 below also apply to any patient who—

(a) does not fall within subsection (3) above;

(b) is not a community patient; and

(c) has not attained the age of 18 years."

(3) In section 61 (review of treatment), in subsection (1)—

(a) before "a report on" insert ", or by virtue of section 62A below in accordance with a Part 4A certificate (within the meaning of that section),", and

(b) in paragraph (a) for "or 21B(2) above renewing the authority for the detention" substitute ", 20A(4) or 21B(2) above in respect".

(4) After section 62 insert—

"62A Treatment on recall of community patient or revocation of order

(1) This section applies where—

(a) a community patient is recalled to hospital under section 17E above; or

(b) a patient is liable to be detained under this Act following the revocation of a community treatment order under section 17F above in respect of him.

(2) For the purposes of section 58(1)(b) above, the patient is to be treated as if he had remained liable to be detained since the making of the community treatment order.

(3) But section 58 above does not apply to treatment given to the patient if—

(a) the certificate requirement is met for the purposes of section 64C or 64E below; or

(b) as a result of section 64B(4) or 64E(4) below, the certificate requirement would not apply (were the patient a community patient not recalled to hospital under section 17E above).

(4) Section 58A above does not apply to treatment given to the patient if there is authority to give the treatment, and the certificate requirement is met, for the purposes of section 64C or 64E below.

(5) In a case where this section applies, the certificate requirement is met only in so far as—

(a) the Part 4A certificate expressly provides that it is appropriate for one or more specified forms of treatment to be given to the patient in that case (subject to such conditions as may be specified); or

(b) a notice having been given under subsection (5) of section 64H below, treatment is authorised by virtue of subsection (8) of that section.

(6) Subsection (5)(a) above shall not preclude the continuation of any treatment, or of treatment under any plan, pending compliance with section 58 or 58A above if the approved clinician in charge of the treatment considers that the discontinuance of the treatment, or of the treatment under the plan, would cause serious suffering to the patient.

(7) In a case where subsection (1)(b) above applies, subsection (3) above only applies pending compliance with section 58 above.

(8) In subsection (5) above—

"Part 4A certificate" has the meaning given in section 64H below; and

"specified", in relation to a Part 4A certificate, means specified in the certificate."

35 Authority to treat

(1) After Part 4 of the 1983 Act, insert the following Part—

"PART 4A

TREATMENT OF COMMUNITY PATIENTS NOT RECALLED TO HOSPITAL

64A Meaning of "relevant treatment"

In this Part of this Act "relevant treatment", in relation to a patient, means medical treatment which—

(a) is for the mental disorder from which the patient is suffering; and

(b) is not a form of treatment to which section 57 above applies.

64B Adult community patients

(1) This section applies to the giving of relevant treatment to a community patient who—

(a) is not recalled to hospital under section 17E above; and

(b) has attained the age of 16 years.

(2) The treatment may not be given to the patient unless—

(a) there is authority to give it to him; and

(b) if it is section 58 type treatment or section 58A type treatment, the certificate requirement is met.

(3) But the certificate requirement does not apply if—

(a) giving the treatment to the patient is authorised in accordance with section 64G below; or

(b) the treatment is immediately necessary and—

(i) the patient has capacity to consent to it and does consent to it; or

(ii) a donee or deputy or the Court of Protection consents to the treatment on the patient's behalf.

(4) Nor does the certificate requirement apply in so far as the administration of medicine to the patient at any time during the period of one month beginning with the day on which the community treatment order is made is section 58 type treatment.

(5) The reference in subsection (4) above to the administration of medicine does not include any form of treatment specified under section 58(1)(a) above.

64C Section 64B: supplemental

(1) This section has effect for the purposes of section 64B above.

(2) There is authority to give treatment to a patient if—

(a) he has capacity to consent to it and does consent to it;

(b) a donee or deputy or the Court of Protection consents to it on his behalf; or

(c) giving it to him is authorised in accordance with section 64D or 64G below.

(3) Relevant treatment is section 58 type treatment or section 58A type treatment if, at the time when it is given to the patient, section 58 or 58A above (respectively) would have applied to it, had the patient remained liable to be detained at that time (rather than being a community patient).

(4) The certificate requirement is met in respect of treatment to be given to a patient if—

(a) a registered medical practitioner appointed for the purposes of Part 4 of this Act (not being the responsible clinician or the person in charge of the treatment) has certified in writing that it is appropriate for the treatment to be given or for the treatment to be given subject to such conditions as may be specified in the certificate; and

(b) if conditions are so specified, the conditions are satisfied.

(5) In a case where the treatment is section 58 type treatment, treatment is immediately necessary if—

(a) it is immediately necessary to save the patient's life; or

(b) it is immediately necessary to prevent a serious deterioration of the patient's condition and is not irreversible; or

(c) it is immediately necessary to alleviate serious suffering by the patient and is not irreversible or hazardous; or

(d) it is immediately necessary, represents the minimum interference necessary to prevent the patient from behaving violently or being a danger to himself or others and is not irreversible or hazardous.

(6) In a case where the treatment is section 58A type treatment by virtue of subsection (1)(a) of that section, treatment is immediately necessary if it falls within paragraph (a) or (b) of subsection (5) above.

(7) In a case where the treatment is section 58A type treatment by virtue of subsection (1)(b) of that section, treatment is immediately necessary if it

falls within such of paragraphs (a) to (d) of subsection (5) above as may be specified in regulations under that section.

(8) For the purposes of subsection (7) above, the regulations—

(a) may make different provision for different cases (and may, in particular, make different provision for different forms of treatment);

(b) may make provision which applies subject to specified exceptions; and

(c) may include transitional, consequential, incidental or supplemental provision.

(9) Subsection (3) of section 62 above applies for the purposes of this section as it applies for the purposes of that section.

64D Adult community patients lacking capacity

(1) A person is authorised to give relevant treatment to a patient as mentioned in section 64C(2)(c) above if the conditions in subsections (2) to (6) below are met.

(2) The first condition is that, before giving the treatment, the person takes reasonable steps to establish whether the patient lacks capacity to consent to the treatment.

(3) The second condition is that, when giving the treatment, he reasonably believes that the patient lacks capacity to consent to it.

(4) The third condition is that—

(a) he has no reason to believe that the patient objects to being given the treatment; or

(b) he does have reason to believe that the patient so objects, but it is not necessary to use force against the patient in order to give the treatment.

(5) The fourth condition is that—

(a) he is the person in charge of the treatment and an approved clinician; or

(b) the treatment is given under the direction of that clinician.

(6) The fifth condition is that giving the treatment does not conflict with—

(a) an advance decision which he is satisfied is valid and applicable; or

(b) a decision made by a donee or deputy or the Court of Protection.

(7) In this section—

(a) reference to an advance decision is to an advance decision (within the meaning of the Mental Capacity Act 2005) made by the patient; and

(b) "valid and applicable", in relation to such a decision, means valid and applicable to the treatment in question in accordance with section 25 of that Act.

64E Child community patients

(1) This section applies to the giving of relevant treatment to a community patient who—

(a) is not recalled to hospital under section 17E above; and

(b) has not attained the age of 16 years.

(2) The treatment may not be given to the patient unless—

(a) there is authority to give it to him; and

(b) if it is section 58 type treatment or section 58A type treatment, the certificate requirement is met.

(3) But the certificate requirement does not apply if—

(a) giving the treatment to the patient is authorised in accordance with section 64G below; or

(b) in a case where the patient is competent to consent to the treatment and does consent to it, the treatment is immediately necessary.

(4) Nor does the certificate requirement apply in so far as the administration of medicine to the patient at any time during the period of one month beginning with the day on which the community treatment order is made is section 58 type treatment.

(5) The reference in subsection (4) above to the administration of medicine does not include any form of treatment specified under section 58(1)(a) above.

(6) For the purposes of subsection (2)(a) above, there is authority to give treatment to a patient if—

(a) he is competent to consent to it and he does consent to it; or

(b) giving it to him is authorised in accordance with section 64F or 64G below.

(7) Subsections (3) to (9) of section 64C above have effect for the purposes of this section as they have effect for the purposes of section 64B above.

(8) Regulations made by virtue of section 32(2)(d) above apply for the purposes of this section as they apply for the purposes of Part 2 of this Act.

64F Child community patients lacking competence

(1) A person is authorised to give relevant treatment to a patient as mentioned in section 64E(6)(b) above if the conditions in subsections (2) to (5) below are met.

(2) The first condition is that, before giving the treatment, the person takes reasonable steps to establish whether the patient is competent to consent to the treatment.

(3) The second condition is that, when giving the treatment, he reasonably believes that the patient is not competent to consent to it.

(4) The third condition is that—

(a) he has no reason to believe that the patient objects to being given the treatment; or

(b) he does have reason to believe that the patient so objects, but it is not necessary to use force against the patient in order to give the treatment.

(5) The fourth condition is that—

(a) he is the person in charge of the treatment and an approved clinician; or

(b) the treatment is given under the direction of that clinician.

64G Emergency treatment for patients lacking capacity or competence

(1) A person is also authorised to give relevant treatment to a patient as mentioned in section 64C(2)(c) or 64E(6)(b) above if the conditions in subsections (2) to (4) below are met.

(2) The first condition is that, when giving the treatment, the person reasonably believes that the patient lacks capacity to consent to it or, as the case may be, is not competent to consent to it.

(3) The second condition is that the treatment is immediately necessary.

(4) The third condition is that if it is necessary to use force against the patient in order to give the treatment—

(a) the treatment needs to be given in order to prevent harm to the patient; and

(b) the use of such force is a proportionate response to the likelihood of the patient's suffering harm, and to the seriousness of that harm.

(5) Subject to subsections (6) to (8) below, treatment is immediately necessary if—

(a) it is immediately necessary to save the patient's life; or

(b) it is immediately necessary to prevent a serious deterioration of the patient's condition and is not irreversible; or

(c) it is immediately necessary to alleviate serious suffering by the patient and is not irreversible or hazardous; or

(d) it is immediately necessary, represents the minimum interference necessary to prevent the patient from behaving violently or being a danger to himself or others and is not irreversible or hazardous.

(6) Where the treatment is section 58A type treatment by virtue of subsection (1)(a) of that section, treatment is immediately necessary if it falls within paragraph (a) or (b) of subsection (5) above.

(7) Where the treatment is section 58A type treatment by virtue of subsection (1)(b) of that section, treatment is immediately necessary if it falls within such of paragraphs (a) to (d) of subsection (5) above as may be specified in regulations under section 58A above.

(8) For the purposes of subsection (7) above, the regulations—

(a) may make different provision for different cases (and may, in particular, make different provision for different forms of treatment);

(b) may make provision which applies subject to specified exceptions; and

(c) may include transitional, consequential, incidental or supplemental provision.

(9) Subsection (3) of section 62 above applies for the purposes of this section as it applies for the purposes of that section.

64H Certificates: supplementary provisions

(1) A certificate under section 64B(2)(b) or 64E(2)(b) above (a "Part 4A certificate") may relate to a plan of treatment under which the patient is to be given (whether within a specified period or otherwise) one or more forms of section 58 type treatment or section 58A type treatment.

(2) A Part 4A certificate shall be in such form as may be prescribed by regulations made by the appropriate national authority.

(3) Before giving a Part 4A certificate, the registered medical practitioner concerned shall consult two other persons who have been professionally concerned with the patient's medical treatment but, of those persons—

(a) at least one shall be a person who is not a registered medical practitioner; and

(b) neither shall be the patient's responsible clinician or the person in charge of the treatment in question.

(4) Where a patient is given treatment in accordance with a Part 4A certificate, a report on the treatment and the patient's condition shall be given by the person in charge of the treatment to the appropriate national authority if required by that authority.

(5) The appropriate national authority may at any time give notice directing that a Part 4A certificate shall not apply to treatment given to a patient after a date specified in the notice, and the relevant section shall then apply to any such treatment as if that certificate had not been given.

(6) The relevant section is—

(a) if the patient is not recalled to hospital in accordance with section 17E above, section 64B or 64E above;

(b) if the patient is so recalled or is liable to be detained under this Act following revocation of the community treatment order under section 17F above—

(i) section 58 above, in the case of section 58 type treatment;

(ii) section 58A above, in the case of section 58A type treatment;

(subject to section 62A(2) above).

(7) The notice under subsection (5) above shall be given to the person in charge of the treatment in question.

(8) Subsection (5) above shall not preclude the continuation of any treatment or of treatment under any plan pending compliance with the relevant section if the person in charge of the treatment considers that the discontinuance of the treatment or of treatment under the plan would cause serious suffering to the patient.

(9) In this section, "the appropriate national authority" means—

(a) in relation to community patients in respect of whom the responsible hospital is in England, the Secretary of State;

(b) in relation to community patients in respect of whom the responsible hospital is in Wales, the Welsh Ministers.

64I Liability for negligence

Nothing in section 64D, 64F or 64G above excludes a person's civil liability for loss or damage, or his criminal liability, resulting from his negligence in doing anything authorised to be done by that section.

64J Factors to be considered in determining whether patient objects to treatment

(1) In assessing for the purposes of this Part whether he has reason to believe that a patient objects to treatment, a person shall consider all the circumstances so far as they are reasonably ascertainable, including the patient's behaviour, wishes, feelings, views, beliefs and values.

(2) But circumstances from the past shall be considered only so far as it is still appropriate to consider them.

64K Interpretation of Part 4A

(1) This Part of this Act is to be construed as follows.

(2) References to a patient who lacks capacity are to a patient who lacks capacity within the meaning of the Mental Capacity Act 2005.

(3) References to a patient who has capacity are to be read accordingly.

(4) References to a donee are to a donee of a lasting power of attorney (within the meaning of section 9 of the Mental Capacity Act 2005) created by the patient, where the donee is acting within the scope of his authority and in accordance with that Act.

(5) References to a deputy are to a deputy appointed for the patient by the Court of Protection under section 16 of the Mental Capacity Act 2005, where the deputy is acting within the scope of his authority and in accordance with that Act.

(6) Reference to the responsible clinician shall be construed as a reference to the responsible clinician within the meaning of Part 2 of this Act.

(7) References to a hospital include a registered establishment.

(8) Section 64(3) above applies for the purposes of this Part of this Act as it applies for the purposes of Part 4 of this Act."

(2) In section 119 of the 1983 Act (practitioners approved for Part 4 and section 118)—

(a) in subsection (2)—

(i) after "those provisions" insert "or under Part 4A of this Act",

(ii) in paragraph (a), for "in a registered establishment" substitute "in a hospital or registered establishment or any community patient in a hospital or establishment of any description or (if access is granted) other place", and

(iii) in paragraph (b), for "in that home" substitute "there", and

(b) after subsection (2) insert—

"(3) In this section, "establishment of any description" shall be construed in accordance with section 4(8) of the Care Standards Act 2000."

(3) In section 121 of the 1983 Act (Mental Health Act Commission), in subsection (2)(b) after "61" insert ", 64H(5)".

(4) The Mental Capacity Act 2005 (c. 9) is amended as follows.

(5) In section 28 (Mental Health Act matters), after subsection (1A) (inserted by section 28 of this Act) insert—

"(1B) Section 5 does not apply to an act to which section 64B of the Mental Health Act applies (treatment of community patients not recalled to hospital)."

(6) In section 37 (independent mental capacity advocates: provision of serious medical treatment by NHS body), in subsection (2) after "Part 4" insert "or 4A".

36 Repeal of provisions for after-care under supervision

(1) The 1983 Act is amended as follows.

(2) Sections 25A to 25J (after-care under supervision) are omitted.

(3) In section 66 (applications to tribunals), in subsection (2)(c), for "cases mentioned in paragraphs (c) and (ga)" substitute "case mentioned in paragraph (c)".

(4) In Part 1 of Schedule 1 (application of certain provisions to patients subject to hospital and guardianship orders: patients not subject to special restrictions), in paragraph 1, for "25C" substitute "26".

CHAPTER 5

MENTAL HEALTH REVIEW TRIBUNALS

37 References

(1) The 1983 Act is amended as follows.

(2) In section 21 (special provision as to patients absent without leave), after subsection (2) insert—

"(3) Where a patient is absent without leave on the day on which (apart from this section) the managers would be required under section 68 below to refer the patient's case to a Mental Health Review Tribunal, that requirement shall not apply unless and until—

(a) the patient is taken into custody under section 18 above and returned to the hospital where he ought to be; or

(b) the patient returns himself to the hospital where he ought to be within the period during which he can be taken into custody under section 18 above."

(3) For section 68 substitute—

"68 Duty of managers of hospitals to refer cases to tribunal

(1) This section applies in respect of the following patients—

(a) a patient who is admitted to a hospital in pursuance of an application for admission for assessment;

(b) a patient who is admitted to a hospital in pursuance of an application for admission for treatment;

(c) a community patient;

(d) a patient whose community treatment order is revoked under section 17F above;

(e) a patient who is transferred from guardianship to a hospital in pursuance of regulations made under section 19 above.

(2) On expiry of the period of six months beginning with the applicable day, the managers of the hospital shall refer the patient's case to a Mental Health Review Tribunal.

(3) But they shall not do so if during that period—

(a) any right has been exercised by or in respect of the patient by virtue of any of paragraphs (b), (ca), (cb), (e), (g) and (h) of section 66(1) above;

(b) a reference has been made in respect of the patient under section 67(1) above, not being a reference made while the patient is or was liable to be detained in pursuance of an application for admission for assessment; or

(c) a reference has been made in respect of the patient under subsection (7) below.

(4) A person who applies to a tribunal but subsequently withdraws his application shall be treated for these purposes as not having exercised his right to apply, and if he withdraws his application on a date after expiry of the period mentioned in subsection (2) above, the managers shall refer the patient's case as soon as possible after that date.

(5) In subsection (2) above, "the applicable day" means—

(a) in the case of a patient who is admitted to a hospital in pursuance of an application for admission for assessment, the day on which the patient was so admitted;

(b) in the case of a patient who is admitted to a hospital in pursuance of an application for admission for treatment—

(i) the day on which the patient was so admitted; or

(ii) if, when he was so admitted, he was already liable to be detained in pursuance of an application for admission for assessment, the day on which he was originally admitted in pursuance of the application for admission for assessment;

(c) in the case of a community patient or a patient whose community treatment order is revoked under section 17F above, the day mentioned in sub-paragraph (i) or (ii), as the case may be, of paragraph (b) above;

(d) in the case of a patient who is transferred from guardianship to a hospital, the day on which he was so transferred.

(6) The managers of the hospital shall also refer the patient's case to a Mental Health Review Tribunal if a period of more than three years (or, if the patient has not attained the age of 18 years, one year) has elapsed since his case was last considered by such a tribunal, whether on his own application or otherwise.

(7) If, in the case of a community patient, the community treatment order is revoked under section 17F above, the managers of the hospital shall also refer the patient's case to a Mental Health Review Tribunal as soon as possible after the order is revoked.

(8) For the purposes of furnishing information for the purposes of a reference under this section, a registered medical practitioner or approved clinician authorised by or on behalf of the patient may at any reasonable time—

(a) visit and examine the patient in private; and

(b) require the production of and inspect any records relating to the detention or treatment of the patient in any hospital or any after-care services provided for him under section 117 below.

(9) Reference in this section to the managers of the hospital—

(a) in relation to a community patient, is to the managers of the responsible hospital;

(b) in relation to any other patient, is to the managers of the hospital in which he is liable to be detained.

68A Power to reduce periods under section 68

(1) The appropriate national authority may from time to time by order amend subsection (2) or (6) of section 68 above so as to substitute for a period mentioned there such shorter period as is specified in the order.

(2) The order may include such transitional, consequential, incidental or supplemental provision as the appropriate national authority thinks fit.

(3) The order may, in particular, make provision for a case where—

(a) a patient in respect of whom subsection (1) of section 68 above applies is, or is about to be, transferred from England to Wales or from Wales to England; and

(b) the period by reference to which subsection (2) or (6) of that section operates for the purposes of the patient's case is not the same in one territory as it is in the other.

(4) A patient is transferred from one territory to the other if—

(a) he is transferred from a hospital, or from guardianship, in one territory to a hospital in the other in pursuance of regulations made under section 19 above;

(b) he is removed under subsection (3) of that section from a hospital or accommodation in one territory to a hospital or accommodation in the other;

(c) he is a community patient responsibility for whom is assigned from a hospital in one territory to a hospital in the other in pursuance of regulations made under section 19A above;

(d) on the revocation of a community treatment order in respect of him under section 17F above he is detained in a hospital in the territory other than the one in which the responsible hospital was situated; or

(e) he is transferred or removed under section 123 below from a hospital in one territory to a hospital in the other.

(5) Provision made by virtue of subsection (3) above may require or authorise the managers of a hospital determined in accordance with the order to refer the patient's case to a Mental Health Review Tribunal.

(6) In so far as making provision by virtue of subsection (3) above, the order—

(a) may make different provision for different cases;

(b) may make provision which applies subject to specified exceptions.

(7) Where the appropriate national authority for one territory makes an order under subsection (1) above, the appropriate national authority for the other territory may by order make such provision in consequence of the order as it thinks fit.

(8) An order made under subsection (7) above may, in particular, make provision for a case within subsection (3) above (and subsections (4) to (6) above shall apply accordingly).

(9) In this section, "the appropriate national authority" means—

(a) in relation to a hospital in England, the Secretary of State;

(b) in relation to a hospital in Wales, the Welsh Ministers."

(4) In section 71 (references by Secretary of State concerning restricted patients), after subsection (3) insert—

"(3A) An order under subsection (3) above may include such transitional, consequential, incidental or supplemental provision as the Secretary of State thinks fit."

(5) In section 143 (general provisions as to regulations, orders and rules)—

(a) in subsection (2)—

(i) after "order made" insert "by the Secretary of State", and

(ii) after "54A" insert "or 68A(7)", and

(b) in subsection (3)—

(i) after "made" insert "by the Secretary of State", and

(ii) for "68(4)" substitute "68A(1)".

(6) In Part 1 of Schedule 1 to that Act (application of certain provisions to patients subject to hospital and guardianship orders: patients not subject to special restrictions)—

(a) in paragraph 2—

(i) for "and 66" substitute ", 66 and 68", and

(ii) for "to 9" substitute "to 10", and

(b) after paragraph 9 insert—

"10 In section 68—

(a) in subsection (1) paragraph (a) shall be omitted; and

(b) subsections (2) to (5) shall apply if the patient falls within paragraph (e) of subsection (1), but not otherwise."

38 Organisation

(1) The 1983 Act is amended as follows.

(2) In section 65 (Mental Health Review Tribunals), for subsections (1) to (1C) substitute—

"(1) There shall be—

(a) a Mental Health Review Tribunal for England; and

(b) a Mental Health Review Tribunal for Wales.

(1A) The purpose of the Mental Health Review Tribunals is to deal with applications and references by and in respect of patients under the provisions of this Act."

(3) In section 78 (procedure of tribunals)—

(a) in subsections (2)(a) and (k) and (6), for "chairman" substitute "President",

(b) in subsection (2)(a), for "any other" substitute "the other",

(c) in subsections (2)(b) and (4)(b), for "another" substitute "the other",

(d) in subsection (4)(a), for "president" substitute "chairman", and

(e) in subsection (6) omit ", if for any reason he is unable to act,".

(4) In section 79 (interpretation of Part 5), for subsection (7) substitute—

"(7) For the purposes of this Part of this Act—

(a) the area of the Mental Health Review Tribunal for England is England; and

(b) the area of the Mental Health Review Tribunal for Wales is Wales."

(5) Schedule 2 (Mental Health Review Tribunals) is amended as set out in subsections (6) to (9).

(6) For paragraph 3 substitute—

"3 (1) The Lord Chancellor shall appoint one of the legal members of the Mental Health Review Tribunal for England to be the President of that tribunal.

(2) The Lord Chancellor shall appoint one of the legal members of the Mental Health Review Tribunal for Wales to be the President of that tribunal."

(7) In paragraph 4—

(a) for "chairman", in each place, substitute "President", and

(b) omit ", if for any reason he is unable to act,".

(8) In paragraph 5—

(a) for "any area" substitute "one area", and

(b) for "any other" substitute "the other".

(9) In paragraph 6—

(a) for "chairman", in each place, substitute "President", and

(b) for "president", in each place, substitute "chairman".

CHAPTER 6

CROSS-BORDER PATIENTS

39 Cross-border arrangements

(1) At the end of section 17 of the 1983 Act (leave of absence) insert—

"(6) Subsection (7) below applies to a person who is granted leave by or by virtue of a provision—

(a) in force in Scotland, Northern Ireland, any of the Channel Islands or the Isle of Man; and

(b) corresponding to subsection (1) above.

(7) For the purpose of giving effect to a direction or condition imposed by virtue of a provision corresponding to subsection (3) above, the person may be conveyed to a place in, or kept in custody or detained at a place of safety in, England and Wales by a person authorised in that behalf by the direction or condition."

(2) Schedule 5 (which contains amendments to Part 6 of the 1983 Act and related amendments) has effect.

CHAPTER 7

RESTRICTED PATIENTS

40 Restriction orders

(1) In section 41(1) of the 1983 Act (restriction orders) omit the words ", either without limit of time or during such period as may be specified in the order".

(2) In section 42(4)(b) of the 1983 Act (powers in respect of patients subject to restriction orders) omit the words from ", and, if the restriction order was made for a specified period," to the end.

(3) In the following provisions omit the words ", made without limitation of time"—

(a) section 44(3) of the 1983 Act (committal to hospital),

(b) section 84(2) of the 1983 Act (removal from Islands), and

(c) section 10(3)(a) of the Colonial Prisoners Removal Act 1884 (c. 31) (criminal lunatics).

(4) In section 81(7) of the 1983 Act (removal to Northern Ireland: expiry of restriction order or direction) omit (in each place) "restriction order or".

(5) In section 81A(3) of the 1983 Act (transfer of responsibility for patient to Northern Ireland: expiry of restriction order or direction)—

(a) omit (in each place) "restriction order or", and
(b) omit "order or".

(6) In section 91(2) of the 1983 Act (patients removed from England and Wales: revival of order on return) omit the words "at any time before the end of the period for which those orders would have continued in force".

(7) But subsections (3) to (6) shall have no effect in respect of—
(a) a restriction order for a specified period made before subsection (1) comes into force, or
(b) an order made outside England and Wales which is treated under the 1983 Act as if it were a restriction order for a specified period.

41 Conditionally discharged patients subject to limitation directions

In section 75(3) of the 1983 Act (power of Mental Health Review Tribunal to direct that restriction order, etc. is to cease to have effect)—
(a) in paragraph (b), after "restriction order", insert ", limitation direction", and
(b) after "hospital order", insert ", hospital direction".

CHAPTER 8

MISCELLANEOUS

42 Offence of ill-treatment: increase in maximum penalty on conviction on indictment

In section 127 of the 1983 Act (ill-treatment or wilful neglect of patients), in subsection (3)(b), for "two years" substitute "five years".

43 Informal admission of patients aged 16 or 17

In section 131 of the 1983 Act (informal admission of patients), for subsection (2) substitute—

"(2) Subsections (3) and (4) below apply in the case of a patient aged 16 or 17 years who has capacity to consent to the making of such arrangements as are mentioned in subsection (1) above.

(3) If the patient consents to the making of the arrangements, they may be made, carried out and determined on the basis of that consent even though there are one or more persons who have parental responsibility for him.

(4) If the patient does not consent to the making of the arrangements, they may not be made, carried out or determined on the basis of the consent of a person who has parental responsibility for him.

(5) In this section—
(a) the reference to a patient who has capacity is to be read in accordance with the Mental Capacity Act 2005; and
(b) "parental responsibility" has the same meaning as in the Children Act 1989."

44 Places of safety

(1) The 1983 Act is amended as follows.

(2) In section 135 (warrant to search for and remove patients), after subsection (3) insert—

"(3A) A constable, an approved mental health professional or a person authorised by either of them for the purposes of this subsection may, before the end of the period of 72 hours mentioned in subsection (3) above, take a person detained in a place of safety under that subsection to one or more other places of safety.

(3B) A person taken to a place of safety under subsection (3A) above may be detained there for a period ending no later than the end of the period of 72 hours mentioned in subsection (3) above."

(3) In section 136 (mentally disordered persons found in public places), after subsection (2) insert—

"(3) A constable, an approved mental health professional or a person authorised by either of them for the purposes of this subsection may, before the end of the period of 72 hours mentioned in subsection (2) above, take a person detained in a place of safety under that subsection to one or more other places of safety.

(4) A person taken to a place of a safety under subsection (3) above may be detained there for a purpose mentioned in subsection (2) above for a period ending no later than the end of the period of 72 hours mentioned in that subsection."

45 Delegation of powers of managers of NHS foundation trusts

(1) In section 23(6) of the 1983 Act (delegation of NHS foundation trust's power to discharge patients), for the words from "non-executive directors" to the end substitute "persons authorised by the board of the trust in that behalf each of whom is neither an executive director of the board nor an employee of the trust."

(2) In section 32(3) of the 1983 Act (power to make provision about how hospital managers' functions under Part 2 of that Act are to be exercised), after "23(4)" insert "and (6)".

(3) After section 142A of the 1983 Act (inserted by section 17 of this Act), insert—

"142B Delegation of powers of managers of NHS foundation trusts

(1) The constitution of an NHS foundation trust may not provide for a function under this Act to be delegated otherwise than in accordance with provision made by or under this Act.

(2) Paragraph 15(3) of Schedule 7 to the National Health Service Act 2006 (which provides that the powers of a public benefit corporation may be delegated to a committee of directors or to an executive director) shall have effect subject to this section."

46 Local Health Boards

(1) The 1983 Act is amended as follows.

(2) In section 19(3) (removal of patients), after "NHS foundation trust", in each place, insert ", Local Health Board".

(3) In section 145(1) (interpretation)—

(a) in the definition of "hospital", after paragraph (b) insert "; and

(c) any hospital as defined by section 206 of the National Health Service (Wales) Act 2006 which is vested in a Local Health Board;", and

(b) in the definition of "the managers", after paragraph (bc) insert—

"(bd) in relation to a hospital vested in a Local Health Board, the Board;".

47 Welsh Ministers: procedure for instruments

(1) Section 143 of the 1983 Act (general provisions as to regulations, orders and rules) is amended as follows.

(2) In subsection (2), for "or rules made" substitute "made by the Secretary of State, or rules made,".

(3) After subsection (3) insert—

"(3A) Subsections (3B) to (3D) apply where power to make regulations or an order under this Act is conferred on the Welsh Ministers (other than by or by virtue of the Government of Wales Act 2006).

(3B) Any power of the Welsh Ministers to make regulations or an order shall be exercisable by statutory instrument.

(3C) Any statutory instrument containing regulations, or an order under section 68A(7) above, made by the Welsh Ministers shall be subject to annulment in pursuance of a resolution of the National Assembly for Wales.

(3D) No order shall be made under section 68A(1) above by the Welsh Ministers unless a draft of it has been approved by a resolution of the National Assembly for Wales.

(3E) In this section—

(a) references to the Secretary of State include the Secretary of State and the Welsh Ministers acting jointly; and

(b) references to the Welsh Ministers include the Welsh Ministers and the Secretary of State acting jointly."

PART 2

AMENDMENTS TO OTHER ACTS

CHAPTER 1

AMENDMENTS TO DOMESTIC VIOLENCE, CRIME AND VICTIMS ACT 2004

48 Victims' rights

Schedule 6 (which makes amendments to Chapter 2 of Part 3 of the Domestic Violence, Crime and Victims Act 2004 (c. 28)) has effect.

CHAPTER 2

AMENDMENTS TO MENTAL CAPACITY ACT 2005

49 Independent mental capacity advocacy service: exceptions

For section 40 of the Mental Capacity Act 2005 (c. 9) (independent mental capacity advocacy service: exceptions) substitute—

"40 Exceptions

The duty imposed by section 37(3), 38(3) or (4) or 39(4) or (5) does not apply where there is—

(a) a person nominated by P (in whatever manner) as a person to be consulted on matters to which that duty relates,

(b) a donee of a lasting power of attorney created by P who is authorised to make decisions in relation to those matters, or

(c) a deputy appointed by the court for P with power to make decisions in relation to those matters."

50 Mental Capacity Act 2005: deprivation of liberty

(1) The Mental Capacity Act 2005 (c. 9) is amended as follows.

(2) After section 4 insert—

"4A Restriction on deprivation of liberty

(1) This Act does not authorise any person ("D") to deprive any other person ("P") of his liberty.

(2) But that is subject to—

(a) the following provisions of this section, and

(b) section 4B.

(3) D may deprive P of his liberty if, by doing so, D is giving effect to a relevant decision of the court.

(4) A relevant decision of the court is a decision made by an order under section 16(2)(a) in relation to a matter concerning P's personal welfare.

(5) D may deprive P of his liberty if the deprivation is authorised by Schedule A1 (hospital and care home residents: deprivation of liberty).

4B Deprivation of liberty necessary for life-sustaining treatment etc

(1) If the following conditions are met, D is authorised to deprive P of his liberty while a decision as respects any relevant issue is sought from the court.

(2) The first condition is that there is a question about whether D is authorised to deprive P of his liberty under section 4A.

(3) The second condition is that the deprivation of liberty—

(a) is wholly or partly for the purpose of—

(i) giving P life-sustaining treatment, or

(ii) doing any vital act, or

(b) consists wholly or partly of—

(i) giving P life-sustaining treatment, or

(ii) doing any vital act.

(4) The third condition is that the deprivation of liberty is necessary in order to—

(a) give the life-sustaining treatment, or

(b) do the vital act.

(5) A vital act is any act which the person doing it reasonably believes to be necessary to prevent a serious deterioration in P's condition."

(3) After section 16 insert—

"16A Section 16 powers: Mental Health Act patients etc

(1) If a person is ineligible to be deprived of liberty by this Act, the court may not include in a welfare order provision which authorises the person to be deprived of his liberty.

(2) If—

(a) a welfare order includes provision which authorises a person to be deprived of his liberty, and

(b) that person becomes ineligible to be deprived of liberty by this Act,

the provision ceases to have effect for as long as the person remains ineligible.

(3) Nothing in subsection (2) affects the power of the court under section 16(7) to vary or discharge the welfare order.

(4) For the purposes of this section—

(a) Schedule 1A applies for determining whether or not P is ineligible to be deprived of liberty by this Act;

(b) "welfare order" means an order under section 16(2)(a)."

(4) Omit the following provisions (which make specific provision about deprivation of liberty)—

(a) section 6(5);
(b) section 11(6);
(c) section 20(13).

(5) Schedule 7 (which inserts the new Schedule A1 into the Mental Capacity Act 2005 (c. 9)) has effect.

(6) Schedule 8 (which inserts the new Schedule 1A into the Mental Capacity Act 2005) has effect.

(7) Schedule 9 (which makes other amendments to the Mental Capacity Act 2005 and to other Acts) has effect.

(8) In subsection (9)—

"GOWA 1998" means the Government of Wales Act 1998 (c. 38);

"GOWA 2006" means the Government of Wales Act 2006 (c. 32);

"initial period" has the same meaning as in Schedule 11 to GOWA 2006.

(9) If this Act is passed after the end of the initial period, the functions conferred on the National Assembly for Wales by virtue of any provision of this Part of this Act are to be treated for the purposes of Schedule 11 to GOWA 2006 as if they—
(a) had been conferred on the Assembly constituted by GOWA 1998 by an Act passed before the end of the initial period, and
(b) were exercisable by that Assembly immediately before the end of the initial period.

(10) If any function of making subordinate legislation conferred by virtue of any provision of this Part of this Act is transferred to the Welsh Ministers (whether by virtue of subsection (9) or otherwise)—
(a) paragraphs 34 and 35 of Schedule 11 to the Government of Wales Act 2006 do not apply; and
(b) subsections (11) and (12) apply instead.

(11) If a relevant statutory instrument contains regulations under paragraph 42(2)(b), 129, 163 or 164 of Schedule A1 to the Mental Capacity Act 2005 (whether or not it also contains other regulations), the instrument may not be made unless a draft has been laid before and approved by resolution of the National Assembly for Wales.

(12) Subject to that, a relevant statutory instrument is subject to annulment in pursuance of a resolution of the National Assembly for Wales.

(13) In subsections (11) and (12) "relevant statutory instrument" means a statutory instrument containing subordinate legislation made in exercise of a function transferred as mentioned in subsection (10).

51 Amendment to section 20(11) of Mental Capacity Act 2005

In section 20 of the Mental Capacity Act 2005 (c. 9) (restrictions on deputies), in subsection (11)(a), for "or" substitute "and".

PART 3

GENERAL

52 Meaning of "1983 Act"

In this Act "the 1983 Act" means the Mental Health Act 1983 (c. 20).

53 Transitional provisions and savings

Schedule 10 (which contains transitional provisions and savings) has effect.

54 Consequential provisions

(1) The Secretary of State may by order made by statutory instrument make supplementary, incidental or consequential provision for the purposes of, in consequence of, or for giving full effect to a provision of this Act.

(2) An order under subsection (1) may, in particular—

(a) amend or repeal any provision of an Act passed before, or in the same Session as, this Act;

(b) amend or revoke any provision of subordinate legislation made before the passing of this Act;

(c) include transitional or saving provision in connection with the coming into force of provision made by the order.

(3) In relation to provision which deals with matters with respect to which functions are exercisable by the Welsh Ministers—

(a) the power under subsection (1) is exercisable by the Secretary of State only with agreement of the Welsh Ministers, and

(b) the power under that subsection is also exercisable by the Welsh Ministers except that provision may not be made by virtue of subsection (2)(a).

(4) The amendments that may be made by virtue of subsection (2) are in addition to those made by or by virtue of any other provision of this Act.

(5) A statutory instrument containing an order under subsection (1) which makes provision by virtue of subsection (2)(a) may not be made unless a draft of the instrument has been laid before and approved by a resolution of each House of Parliament.

(6) A statutory instrument containing any other order under subsection (1) made by the Secretary of State is subject to annulment in pursuance of a resolution of either House of Parliament.

(7) A statutory instrument containing an order under subsection (1) made by the Welsh Ministers is subject to annulment in pursuance of a resolution of the National Assembly for Wales.

(8) In subsection (2), "subordinate legislation" has the same meaning as in the Interpretation Act 1978 (c. 30).

55 Repeals and revocations

The enactments mentioned in Schedule 11 are repealed or revoked to the extent specified.

56 Commencement

(1) This Act (other than sections 51 to 53 (and Schedule 10), this section and sections 57 to 59) comes into force in accordance with provision made by the Secretary of State by order made by statutory instrument.

(2) In relation to provision which deals with matters with respect to which functions are exercisable by the Welsh Ministers, the power under subsection (1) is exercisable only with their agreement.

(3) Section 51 comes into force in accordance with provision made by the Lord Chancellor by order made by statutory instrument.

(4) An order under this section may—

(a) make different provision for different purposes (including different provision for different areas and different provision for different descriptions of patient);

(b) include transitional or saving provision.

(5) The provision which may be made by virtue of subsection (4)(b) includes provision modifying the application of a provision of this Act pending the commencement of a provision of another enactment.

(6) A statutory instrument containing an order under this section which makes provision by virtue of subsection (4)(b) (including provision within section 57) is subject to annulment in pursuance of a resolution of either House of Parliament.

57 Commencement of section 36

(1) An order under section 56 providing for the commencement of section 36 may, in particular, provide—

(a) for that section not to apply to or affect a patient who is subject to after-care under supervision immediately before that commencement, and

(b) for the patient to cease to be subject to after-care under supervision, and for his case to be dealt with, in accordance with provision made by the order.

(2) The order may require—

(a) a Primary Care Trust or Local Health Board to secure that the patient is examined by a registered medical practitioner of a description specified in the order;

(b) the registered medical practitioner to examine the patient with a view to making a decision about his case by reference to criteria specified in the order.

(3) The order may require the registered medical practitioner, having complied with provision made by virtue of subsection (2)(b)—

(a) to discharge the patient,

(b) to recommend that he be detained in hospital,

(c) to recommend that he be received into guardianship, or

(d) to make a community treatment order in respect of him.

(4) The order may, in respect of a recommendation made by virtue of subsection (3)(b) or (c)—

(a) provide that the recommendation is to be made to a local social services authority determined in accordance with the order;

(b) provide that the recommendation is to be made in accordance with any other requirements specified in the order;

(c) require the local social services authority determined in accordance with paragraph (a), in response to the recommendation, to make arrangements for an approved mental health professional to consider the patient's case on their behalf.

(5) The order may provide that a registered medical practitioner shall not make a community treatment order in respect of a patient unless an approved mental health professional states in writing—

(a) that he agrees with the decision made by the practitioner about the patient's case, and

(b) that it is appropriate to make the order.

(6) An order requiring a registered medical practitioner to make a community treatment order in respect of a patient shall include provision about—

(a) the effect of the community treatment order (in particular, replacing after-care under supervision with a contingent requirement to attend, and be detained at, a hospital), and

(b) the effect of its revocation (including, in particular, provision for detention under section 3 of the 1983 Act).

(7) The order may modify a provision of the 1983 Act in its application in relation to a patient who is subject to after-care under supervision immediately before the commencement of section 36.

(8) Provision made by virtue of subsection (7) may, in particular—

(a) modify any of sections 25A to 25J of the 1983 Act in their application in relation to a patient for so long as he is, by virtue of subsection (1)(a), subject to after-care under supervision after the commencement of section 36;

(b) modify any of sections 17A to 17G, 20A and 20B of that Act (inserted by section 32 of this Act) in their application in relation to a patient in respect of whom a community treatment order is made by virtue of subsection (3)(d).

(9) A reference in this section to section 36 includes the amendments and repeals in Schedules 3 and 11 consequential on that section.

(10) An expression used in this section and in the 1983 Act has the same meaning in this section as it has in that Act.

58 Extent

(1) The provisions of this Act which amend other enactments have the same extent as the enactments which they amend.

(2) But subsection (1) is subject to—

(a) paragraph 35 of Schedule 3,

(b) paragraphs 3, 4 and 20 of Schedule 5, and

(c) paragraph 12 of Schedule 9.

(3) Section 54 extends to the United Kingdom.

59 Short title

This Act may be cited as the Mental Health Act 2007.

SCHEDULES

SCHEDULE 1

Section 1

CATEGORIES OF MENTAL DISORDER: FURTHER AMENDMENTS ETC

PART 1

AMENDMENTS TO 1983 ACT

1 The 1983 Act is amended as follows.

2 In section 3(2) (grounds for application for admission for treatment), in paragraph (a), for "mental illness, severe mental impairment, psychopathic disorder or mental impairment and his mental disorder is" substitute "mental disorder".

3 In section 7(2) (grounds for guardianship application), in paragraph (a), omit the words ", being mental illness, severe mental impairment, psychopathic disorder or mental impairment and his mental disorder is".

4 In section 20 (renewal of detention or guardianship)—

(a) in subsection (4)(a), for "mental illness, severe mental impairment, psychopathic disorder or mental impairment, and his mental disorder is" substitute "mental disorder", and

(b) in subsection (7)(a), for "mental illness, severe mental impairment, psychopathic disorder or mental impairment and his mental disorder is" substitute "mental disorder".

5 In section 35(3) (conditions for exercise of power to remand accused to hospital for report), in paragraph (a), for "mental illness, psychopathic disorder, severe mental impairment or mental impairment" substitute "mental disorder".

6 In section 36(1) (conditions for exercise of power to remand accused to hospital for medical treatment), for the words from "he is suffering" to the end substitute—

"(a) he is suffering from mental disorder of a nature or degree which makes it appropriate for him to be detained in a hospital for medical treatment;".

7 In section 37 (power to order hospital admission or guardianship)—

(a) in subsection (2)(a), for "mental illness, psychopathic disorder, severe mental impairment or mental impairment" substitute "mental disorder", and

(b) in subsection (3), omit the words "as being a person suffering from mental illness or severe mental impairment".

8 In section 38(1) (conditions for exercise of power to make interim hospital order), in paragraph (a), for "mental illness, psychopathic disorder, severe mental impairment or mental impairment" substitute "mental disorder".

9 In section 45A(2) (conditions for exercise of power to direct hospital admission), in paragraph (a), for "psychopathic disorder" substitute "mental disorder".

10 In section 47(1) (power to make transfer direction), in paragraph (a), for "mental illness, psychopathic disorder, severe mental impairment or mental impairment" substitute "mental disorder".

11 In section 48 (further power to make transfer direction)—

(a) in subsection (1), for the words from "that person is suffering" to "such treatment," substitute—

"(a) that person is suffering from mental disorder of a nature or degree which makes it appropriate for him to be detained in a hospital for medical treatment; and

(b) he is in urgent need of such treatment;", and

(b) in subsection (3), for "to (4)" substitute "and (3)".

12 In section 51(6) (further power to make hospital order), in paragraph (a), for the words from "the detainee" to the end substitute—

"(i) the detainee is suffering from mental disorder of a nature or degree which makes it appropriate for the patient to be detained in a hospital for medical treatment;".

13 In section 66(2) (time limits for applications to tribunals), in paragraph (d), for "in the cases mentioned in paragraphs (d), (fb), (g)" substitute "in the case mentioned in paragraph (g)".

14 In section 72 (powers of tribunals)—

(a) in subsection (1)(b)(i), for "mental illness, psychopathic disorder, severe mental impairment or mental impairment or from any of those forms of disorder" substitute "mental disorder or from mental disorder",

(b) in subsection (4)(a), for "mental illness, psychopathic disorder, severe mental impairment or mental impairment" substitute "mental disorder", and

(c) in subsection (6), for "(5)" substitute "(4)".

15 (1) Section 86 (application of power to remove alien patients) is amended as follows.

(2) In subsection (1), for "mental illness" substitute "mental disorder".

(3) After subsection (3) insert—

"(4) In relation to a patient receiving treatment in a hospital within the meaning of the Mental Health (Northern Ireland) Order 1986, the reference in subsection (1) above to mental disorder shall be construed in accordance with that Order."

16 (1) Section 141 (Members of Parliament etc) is amended as follows.

(2) In subsection (1)—

(a) after "House of Commons is authorised to be detained" insert "under a relevant enactment", and

(b) for "mental illness" substitute "mental disorder".

(3) In subsection (4)—

(a) for "mental illness" substitute "mental disorder", and

(b) after "detained" insert "under a relevant enactment".

(4) In subsections (5) and (6), for "mental illness" substitute "mental disorder".

(5) After subsection (6) insert—

"(6A) For the purposes of this section, the following are relevant enactments—

(a) this Act;

(b) the Criminal Procedure (Scotland) Act 1995 and the Mental Health (Care and Treatment) Scotland Act 2003 ("the Scottish enactments"); and

(c) the Mental Health (Northern Ireland) Order 1986 ("the 1986 Order").

(6B) In relation to an authorisation for detention under the Scottish enactments or the 1986 Order, the references in this section to mental disorder shall be construed in accordance with those enactments or that Order (as the case may be)."

17 In section 145(1) (interpretation), for the definitions of "mental disorder", "severe mental impairment", "mental impairment" and "psychopathic disorder" substitute—

""mental disorder" has the meaning given in section 1 above (subject to sections 86(4) and 141(6B));".

PART 2

AMENDMENTS TO OTHER ACTS

Juries Act 1974

18 (1) Part 1 of Schedule 1 to the Juries Act 1974 (c. 23) (mentally disordered persons) is amended as follows.

(2) In paragraph 1, for "mental illness, psychopathic disorder, mental handicap or severe mental handicap" substitute "mental disorder within the meaning of the Mental Health Act 1983".

(3) Omit paragraph 4(1).

Contempt of Court Act 1981

19 In section 14 of the Contempt of Court Act 1981 (c. 49) (proceedings in England and Wales), in subsection (4) and the first subsection (4A), for "mental illness or severe mental impairment" substitute "mental disorder within the meaning of that Act".

Family Law Act 1996

20 (1) The Family Law Act 1996 (c. 27) is amended as follows.

(2) In section 48 (remand for medical examination and report), in subsection (4)—

(a) for "mental illness or severe mental impairment" substitute "mental disorder within the meaning of the Mental Health Act 1983",

(b) for "the Mental Health Act 1983" substitute "that Act", and

(c) for "section 35 of the Act of 1983" substitute "that section".

(3) In section 51 (power of magistrates' court to order hospital admission or guardianship), in subsection (1), for "mental illness or severe mental impairment" substitute "mental disorder within the meaning of that Act".

Housing Act 1996

21 In section 156 of the Housing Act 1996 (c. 52) (remand for medical examination and report), in subsection (4)—

(a) for "mental illness or severe mental impairment" substitute "mental disorder within the meaning of the Mental Health Act 1983",

(b) for "the Mental Health Act 1983" substitute "that Act", and

(c) for "section 35 of that Act" substitute "that section".

Care Standards Act 2000

22 In section 121 of the Care Standards Act 2000 (c. 14) (general interpretation), in subsection (1), for the definition of "mental disorder" substitute—

""mental disorder" has the same meaning as in the Mental Health Act 1983;".

Mental Capacity Act 2005

23 (1) In Schedule 4 to the Mental Capacity Act 2005 (c. 9) (provisions applying to existing enduring powers of attorney), paragraph 23 is amended as follows.

(2) In sub-paragraph (1), omit the words "(within the meaning of the Mental Health Act)".

(3) After sub-paragraph (1) insert—

"(1A) In sub-paragraph (1), "mental disorder" has the same meaning as in the Mental Health Act but disregarding the amendments made to that Act by the Mental Health Act 2007."

National Health Service Act 2006

24 In section 275 of the National Health Service Act 2006 (c. 41) (interpretation), in the definition of "illness" in subsection (1), for "mental disorder within the meaning of the Mental Health Act 1983" substitute "any disorder or disability of the mind".

National Health Service (Wales) Act 2006

25 In section 206 of the National Health Service (Wales) Act 2006 (c. 42) (interpretation), in the definition of "illness" in subsection (1), for "mental disorder within the meaning of the Mental Health Act 1983" substitute "any disorder or disability of the mind".

Police and Justice Act 2006

26 In section 27 of the Police and Justice Act 2006 (c. 48) (anti-social behaviour injunctions: power of arrest and remand), in subsection (11)—

(a) for "mental illness or severe mental impairment" substitute "mental disorder within the meaning of the Mental Health Act 1983", and

(b) for "the Mental Health Act 1983 (c. 20)" substitute "that Act".

SCHEDULE 2

Section 21

APPROVED MENTAL HEALTH PROFESSIONALS: FURTHER AMENDMENTS TO 1983 ACT

1 The 1983 Act is amended as follows.

2 In the following provisions, for "approved social worker" substitute "approved mental health professional"—

(a) section 4(2) (admission for assessment in cases of emergency), and

(b) section 8(1)(c) (effect of guardianship application).

3 (1) Section 10 (transfer of guardianship) is amended as follows.

(2) In subsection (3), for "approved social worker" substitute "approved mental health professional acting on behalf of the local social services authority".

(3) After subsection (4) insert—

"(5) In this section "the local social services authority", in relation to a person (other than a local social services authority) who is the guardian of a patient, means the local social services authority for the area in which that person resides (or resided immediately before his death)."

4 (1) Section 11 (general provisions as to applications) is amended as follows.

(2) In subsection (1), for "approved social worker" substitute "approved mental health professional".

(3) In subsection (3), for "approved social worker, that social worker" substitute "approved mental health professional, that professional".

(4) For subsection (4) substitute—

"(4) An approved mental health professional may not make an application for admission for treatment or a guardianship application in respect of a patient in either of the following cases—

(a) the nearest relative of the patient has notified that professional, or the local social services authority on whose behalf the professional is acting, that he objects to the application being made; or

(b) that professional has not consulted the person (if any) appearing to be the nearest relative of the patient, but the requirement to consult that person does not apply if it appears to the professional that in the circumstances such consultation is not reasonably practicable or would involve unreasonable delay."

5 (1) Section 13 (the title to which becomes "Duty of approved mental health professionals to make applications for admission or guardianship") is amended as follows.

(2) For subsection (1) substitute—

"(1) If a local social services authority have reason to think that an application for admission to hospital or a guardianship application may need to be made in respect of a patient within their area, they shall make arrangements for an approved mental health professional to consider the patient's case on their behalf.

(1A) If that professional is—

(a) satisfied that such an application ought to be made in respect of the patient; and

(b) of the opinion, having regard to any wishes expressed by relatives of the patient or any other relevant circumstances, that it is necessary or proper for the application to be made by him,

he shall make the application.

(1B) Subsection (1C) below applies where—

(a) a local social services authority makes arrangements under subsection (1) above in respect of a patient;

(b) an application for admission for assessment is made under subsection (1A) above in respect of the patient;

(c) while the patient is liable to be detained in pursuance of that application, the authority have reason to think that an application for admission for treatment may need to be made in respect of the patient; and

(d) the patient is not within the area of the authority.

(1C) Where this subsection applies, subsection (1) above shall be construed as requiring the authority to make arrangements under that subsection in place of the authority mentioned there."

(3) In subsection (2), for "approved social worker" substitute "approved mental health professional".

(4) For subsection (3) substitute—

"(3) An application under subsection (1A) above may be made outside the area of the local social services authority on whose behalf the approved mental health professional is considering the patient's case."

(5) In subsection (4)—

(a) for the words from "direct" to "above" substitute "make arrangements under subsection (1) above for an approved mental health professional to consider the patient's case", and

(b) for "that approved social worker" substitute "that professional".

(6) In subsection (5)—

(a) for "approved social worker", in each place, substitute "approved mental health professional", and

(b) after "the power of" insert "a local social services authority to make arrangements with an approved mental health professional to consider a patient's case or of".

6 In section 14 (social reports), for "a social worker" substitute "an approved mental health professional".

7 In the following provisions, for "approved social worker" substitute "approved mental health professional"—

(a) section 18(1) (return of patients absent without leave),

(b) section 21B(3)(b) (consultation before furnishing report),

(c) section 29(2)(c) (application for appointment of acting nearest relative),

(d) section 30(2) (application for variation of orders under section 29),

(e) section 40(1)(a) (power to convey patient),

(f) section 87(1) (power to take Northern Ireland patient into custody),

(g) section 88(3) (power to take England and Wales patient into custody), in the first place it occurs, and

(h) section 89(1) (power to take Channel Islands or Isle of Man patient into custody).

8 For section 115 substitute—

"115 Powers of entry and inspection

"115 "115 Powers of entry and inspection

(1) An approved mental health professional may at all reasonable times enter and inspect any premises (other than a hospital) in which a mentally disordered patient is living, if he has reasonable cause to believe that the patient is not under proper care.

(2) The power under subsection (1) above shall be exercisable only after the professional has produced, if asked to do so, some duly authenticated document showing that he is an approved mental health professional."

9 In section 118(1)(a) (application of code of practice), for "approved social workers" substitute "approved mental health professionals".

10 In the following provisions, for "approved social worker" substitute "approved mental health professional"—

(a) section 135(1) and (4) (warrant to search for and remove patient),

(b) section 136(2) (detention of person removed to a place of safety), and

(c) section 138(1)(a) (retaking of patients escaping from custody).

11 (1) Section 145 (interpretation) is amended as follows.

(2) In subsection (1), for the definition of "approved social worker" substitute—

""“approved mental health professional" has the meaning given in section 114 above;".

(3) After subsection (1AB) (inserted by section 4 of this Act) insert—

"(1AC) References in this Act to an approved mental health professional shall be construed as references to an approved mental health professional acting on behalf of a local social services authority, unless the context otherwise requires."

SCHEDULE 3

Section 32

SUPERVISED COMMUNITY TREATMENT: FURTHER AMENDMENTS TO 1983 ACT

1 The 1983 Act is amended as follows.

Application in respect of patient already in hospital

2 In section 5 (application in respect of patient already in hospital), in subsection (6) after "this Act", in each place, insert "or a community patient".

Return of patients absent without leave

3 (1) Section 18 (return and readmission of patients absent without leave) is amended as follows.

(2) After subsection (2) insert—

"(2A) Where a community patient is at any time absent from a hospital to which he is recalled under section 17E above, he may, subject to the provisions of this section, be taken into custody and returned to the hospital by any approved mental health professional, by any officer on the staff of the hospital, by any constable, or by any person authorised in writing by the responsible clinician or the managers of the hospital."

(3) In subsection (4)—

(a) in paragraph (b), after "guardianship" insert "or, in the case of a community patient, the community treatment order is in force", and

(b) omit the words from "and, in determining" to the end.

(4) After subsection (4) insert—

"(4A) In determining for the purposes of subsection (4)(b) above or any other provision of this Act whether a person who is or has been absent without leave is at any time liable to be detained or subject to guardianship, a report furnished under section 20 or 21B below before the first day of his absence without leave shall not be taken to have renewed the authority for his detention or guardianship unless the period of renewal began before that day.

(4B) Similarly, in determining for those purposes whether a community treatment order is at any time in force in respect of a person who is or has been absent without leave, a report furnished under section 20A or 21B below before the first day of his absence without leave shall not be taken to have extended the community treatment period unless the extension began before that day."

(5) After subsection (6) insert—

"(7) In relation to a patient who has yet to comply with a requirement imposed by virtue of this Act to be in a hospital or place, references in this Act to his liability to be returned to the hospital or place shall include his liability to be taken to that hospital or place; and related expressions shall be construed accordingly."

Assignment of responsibility for community patients

4 After section 19 insert—

"19A Regulations as to assignment of responsibility for community patients

"19A Regulations as to assignment of responsibility for community patients

(1) Responsibility for a community patient may be assigned to another hospital in such circumstances and subject to such conditions as may be prescribed by regulations made by the Secretary of State (if the responsible hospital is in England) or the Welsh Ministers (if that hospital is in Wales).

(2) If responsibility for a community patient is assigned to another hospital—

(a) the application for admission for treatment in respect of the patient shall have effect (subject to section 17D above) as if it had always specified that other hospital;

(b) the patient shall be treated as if he had been admitted to that other hospital at the time when he was originally admitted in pursuance of the application (and as if he had subsequently been discharged under section 17A above from there); and

(c) that other hospital shall become "the responsible hospital" in relation to the patient for the purposes of this Act."

Renewal of authority to detain patients

5 In section 20 (duration of authority)—

(a) in subsection (2), after "discharged" insert "under section 23 below", and

(b) in subsections (3) and (6), after "discharge the patient" insert "under section 23 below".

Special provisions as to patients absent without leave

6 (1) Section 21 (special provisions as to patients absent without leave) is amended as follows.

(2) In subsection (1)—

(a) in paragraph (a), after "Act" insert "or, in the case of a community patient, the community treatment order would cease to be in force", and

(b) after "liable or subject" insert ", or the order shall not cease to be in force,".

(3) After subsection (3) (inserted by section 37 of this Act) insert—

"(4) Where a community patient is absent without leave on the day on which (apart from this section) the 72-hour period mentioned in section 17F above would expire, that period shall not expire until the end of the period of 72 hours beginning with the time when—

(a) the patient is taken into custody under section 18 above and returned to the hospital where he ought to be; or

(b) the patient returns himself to the hospital where he ought to be within the period during which he can be taken into custody under section 18 above.

(5) Any reference in this section, or in sections 21A to 22 below, to the time when a community treatment order would cease, or would have ceased, to

be in force shall be construed as a reference to the time when it would cease, or would have ceased, to be in force by reason only of the passage of time."

7 In section 21A (patients who are taken into custody or return within 28 days), after subsection (3) insert—

"(4) In the case of a community patient, where the period for which the community treatment order is in force is extended by section 21 above, any examination and report to be made and furnished in respect of the patient under section 20A(4) above may be made and furnished within the period as so extended.

(5) Where the community treatment period is extended by virtue of subsection (4) above after the day on which (apart from section 21 above) the order would have ceased to be in force, the extension shall take effect as from that day."

8 (1) Section 21B (patients who are taken into custody or return after more than 28 days) is amended as follows.

(2) In subsection (2), after "ought to be" insert "(his "return day")".

(3) In subsection (3), after "detained" insert "or is a community patient".

(4) For subsection (4) substitute—

"(4) Where—

(a) the patient would (apart from any renewal of the authority for his detention or guardianship on or after his return day) be liable to be detained or subject to guardianship after the end of the period of one week beginning with that day; or

(b) in the case of a community patient, the community treatment order would (apart from any extension of the community treatment period on or after that day) be in force after the end of that period,

he shall cease to be so liable or subject, or the community treatment period shall be deemed to expire, at the end of that period unless a report is duly furnished in respect of him under subsection (2) above."

(5) After subsection (4) insert—

"(4A) If, in the case of a community patient, the community treatment order is revoked under section 17F above during the period of one week beginning with his return day—

(a) subsections (2) and (4) above shall not apply; and

(b) any report already furnished in respect of him under subsection (2) above shall be of no effect."

(6) After subsection (6) insert—

"(6A) In the case of a community patient, where the community treatment order would (apart from section 21 above) have ceased to be in force on or before the day on which a report is duly furnished in respect of him under subsection (2) above, the report shall extend the community treatment period for the period prescribed in that case by section 20A(3) above.

(6B) Where the community treatment period is extended by virtue of subsection (6A) above—

(a) the extension shall take effect as from the day on which (apart from section 21 above and that subsection) the order would have ceased to be in force; and

(b) if (apart from this paragraph) the period as so extended would expire on or before the day on which the report is furnished, the report shall further extend that period, as from the day on which it would expire, for the period prescribed in that case by section 20A(3) above."

(7) After subsection (7) insert—

"(7A) In the case of a community patient, where the community treatment order would (taking account of any extension under subsection (6A) above) cease to be in force within the period of two months beginning with the day on which a report is duly furnished in respect of him under subsection (2) above, the report shall, if it so provides, have effect also as a report duly furnished under section 20A(4) above."

(8) In subsection (10)—

(a) for the definition of "the appropriate body" substitute—

""the appropriate body" means—

(a) in relation to a patient who is liable to be detained in a hospital, the managers of the hospital;

(b) in relation to a patient who is subject to guardianship, the responsible local social services authority;

(c) in relation to a community patient, the managers of the responsible hospital; and", and

(b) for the definition of "the relevant conditions" substitute—

""the relevant conditions" means—

(a) in relation to a patient who is liable to be detained in a hospital, the conditions set out in subsection (4) of section 20 above;

(b) in relation to a patient who is subject to guardianship, the conditions set out in subsection (7) of that section;

(c) in relation to a community patient, the conditions set out in section 20A(6) above."

Patients sentenced to imprisonment etc

9 For section 22 substitute—

"22 Special provisions as to patients sentenced to imprisonment, etc

"22 Special provisions as to patients sentenced to imprisonment, etc

(1) If—

(a) a qualifying patient is detained in custody in pursuance of any sentence or order passed or made by a court in the United Kingdom (including an order committing or remanding him in custody); and

(b) he is so detained for a period exceeding, or for successive periods exceeding in the aggregate, six months,

the relevant application shall cease to have effect on expiry of that period.

(2) A patient is a qualifying patient for the purposes of this section if—

(a) he is liable to be detained by virtue of an application for admission for treatment;

(b) he is subject to guardianship by virtue of a guardianship application; or

(c) he is a community patient.

(3) "The relevant application", in relation to a qualifying patient, means—

(a) in the case of a patient who is subject to guardianship, the guardianship application in respect of him;

(b) in any other case, the application for admission for treatment in respect of him.

(4) The remaining subsections of this section shall apply if a qualifying patient is detained in custody as mentioned in subsection (1)(a) above but for a period not exceeding, or for successive periods not exceeding in the aggregate, six months.

(5) If apart from this subsection—

(a) the patient would have ceased to be liable to be detained or subject to guardianship by virtue of the relevant application on or before the day on which he is discharged from custody; or

(b) in the case of a community patient, the community treatment order would have ceased to be in force on or before that day,

he shall not cease and shall be deemed not to have ceased to be so liable or subject, or the order shall not cease and shall be deemed not to have ceased to be in force, until the end of that day.

(6) In any case (except as provided in subsection (8) below), sections 18, 21 and 21A above shall apply in relation to the patient as if he had absented himself without leave on that day.

(7) In its application by virtue of subsection (6) above section 18 above shall have effect as if—

(a) in subsection (4) for the words from "later of" to the end there were substituted "end of the period of 28 days beginning with the first day of his absence without leave"; and

(b) subsections (4A) and (4B) were omitted.

(8) In relation to a community patient who was not recalled to hospital under section 17E above at the time when his detention in custody began—

(a) section 18 above shall not apply; but

(b) sections 21 and 21A above shall apply as if he had absented himself without leave on the day on which he is discharged from custody and had returned himself as provided in those sections on the last day of the period of 28 days beginning with that day."

Discharge

10 (1) Section 23 (discharge of patients) is amended as follows.

(2) In subsection (1) for the words from "from detention" to the end substitute "absolutely from detention or guardianship is made in accordance with this section".

(3) After subsection (1) insert—

"(1A) Subject to the provisions of this section and section 25 below, a community patient shall cease to be liable to recall under this Part of this Act, and the application for admission for treatment cease to have effect, if an order in writing discharging him from such liability is made in accordance with this section.

(1B) An order under subsection (1) or (1A) above shall be referred to in this Act as "an order for discharge"."

(4) In subsection (2), after paragraph (b) insert—

"(c) where the patient is a community patient, by the responsible clinician, by the managers of the responsible hospital or by the nearest relative of the patient."

(5) In subsection (3)—

(a) for the words from "is liable" to "treatment" substitute "falls within subsection (3A) below", and

(b) for "the patient is maintained" substitute "arrangements have been made in respect of the patient".

(6) After subsection (3) insert—

"(3A) A patient falls within this subsection if—

(a) he is liable to be detained in a registered establishment in pursuance of an application for admission for assessment or for treatment; or

(b) he is a community patient and the responsible hospital is a registered establishment."

11 (1) Section 24 (visiting and examination of patients) is amended as follows.

(2) In subsection (1), after "this Act" insert ", or who is a community patient,".

(3) In subsection (3)—

(a) for the words from ", in respect of" to "his discharge" substitute "any power under section 23(3) above to make an order for a patient's discharge", and

(b) in paragraph (b) for "the home" substitute "the establishment in question".

(4) In subsection (4)—

(a) after "the detention of the patient" insert ", or (as the case may be) for his liability to recall," and

(b) for "the home" substitute "the establishment".

12 (1) Section 25 (restrictions on discharge by nearest relative) is amended as follows.

(2) In subsection (1), after "shall not be made" insert "under section 23 above".

(3) After that subsection insert—

"(1A) Subsection (1) above shall apply to an order for the discharge of a community patient as it applies to an order for the discharge of a patient who is liable to be detained in a hospital, but with the reference to the managers of the hospital being read as a reference to the managers of the responsible hospital."

(4) In subsection (2), after "treatment" insert ", or in respect of a community patient,".

Orders appointing acting nearest relative

13 In section 29 (appointment by court of acting nearest relative), in subsection (3)(d) omit the words "from hospital or guardianship".

14 (1) Section 30 (discharge and variation of orders under section 29) is amended as follows.

(2) In subsection (4), for paragraphs (a) and (b) substitute—

"(a) if—

(i) on the date of the order the patient was liable to be detained or subject to guardianship by virtue of a relevant application, order or direction; or

(ii) he becomes so liable or subject within the period of three months beginning with that date; or

(iii) he was a community patient on the date of the order,

it shall cease to have effect when he is discharged under section 23 above or 72 below or the relevant application, order or direction otherwise ceases to have effect (except as a result of his being transferred in pursuance of regulations under section 19 above);

(b) otherwise, it shall cease to have effect at the end of the period of three months beginning with the date of the order."

(3) After subsection (4) insert—

"(4A) In subsection (4) above, reference to a relevant application, order or direction is to any of the following—

(a) an application for admission for treatment;

(b) a guardianship application;

(c) an order or direction under Part 3 of this Act (other than under section 35, 36 or 38)."

Regulations for purposes of Part 2

15 In section 32 (regulations for purposes of Part 2), in subsection (2)(c) after "this Part of this Act" insert "or community patients".

Wards of court

16 (1) Section 33 (special provisions as to wards of court) is amended as follows.

(2) In subsection (2), after "admission under this Part of this Act" insert "or is a community patient".

(3) For subsection (4) substitute—

"(4) Where a community treatment order has been made in respect of a minor who is a ward of court, the provisions of this Part of this Act relating to community treatment orders and community patients have effect in relation to the minor subject to any order which the court makes in the exercise of its wardship jurisdiction; but this does not apply as regards any period when the minor is recalled to hospital under section 17E above."

Restricted patients

17 In section 41 (power of higher courts to restrict discharge from hospital), in subsection (3)(aa) for "after-care under supervision" substitute "community treatment orders and community patients".

Applications and references to Mental Health Review Tribunal

18 (1) Section 66 (applications to tribunals) is amended as follows.

(2) In subsection (1)—

(a) after paragraph (c) insert—

"(ca) a community treatment order is made in respect of a patient; or

(cb) a community treatment order is revoked under section 17F above in respect of a patient; or",

(b) in paragraph (f), after "discharged" insert "under section 23 above",

(c) after that paragraph insert—

"(fza) a report is furnished under section 20A above in respect of a patient and the patient is not discharged under section 23 above; or",

(d) after paragraph (fa) insert—

"(faa) a report is furnished under subsection (2) of section 21B above in respect of a community patient and subsection (6A) of that section applies (or subsections (6A) and (6B)(b) of that section apply) in the case of the report; or",

(e) in paragraph (g), after "treatment" insert "or a community patient", and

(f) in paragraph (h), after "this Act" insert "or who is a community patient".

(3) In subsection (2)—

(a) after paragraph (c) insert—

"(ca) in the case mentioned in paragraph (ca) of that subsection, six months beginning with the day on which the community treatment order is made;

(cb) in the case mentioned in paragraph (cb) of that subsection, six months beginning with the day on which the community treatment order is revoked;", and

(b) after paragraph (f) insert—

"(fza) in the cases mentioned in paragraphs (fza) and (faa) of that subsection, the period or periods for which the community treatment period is extended by virtue of the report;".

(4) After subsection (2) insert—

"(2A) Nothing in subsection (1)(b) above entitles a community patient to make an application by virtue of that provision even if he is admitted to a hospital on being recalled there under section 17E above."

19 In section 67 (references to tribunals by Secretary of State concerning Part 2 patients), in subsection (1), at the end insert "or of any community patient".

20 In section 69 (applications to tribunals concerning patients subject to hospital and guardianship orders)—

(a) in subsection (1), for paragraph (a) substitute—

"(a) in respect of a patient liable to be detained in pursuance of a hospital order or a community patient who was so liable immediately before he became a community patient, by the nearest relative of the patient in any period in which an application may be made by the patient under any such provision as so applied;",

(b) in subsection (2)(b), omit the words "45B(2), 46(3),", and

(c) after subsection (2) insert—

"(3) The provisions of section 66 above as applied by section 40(4) above are subject to subsection (4) below.

(4) If the initial detention period has not elapsed when the relevant application period begins, the right of a hospital order patient to make an application by virtue of paragraph (ca) or (cb) of section 66(1) above shall be exercisable only during whatever remains of the relevant application period after the initial detention period has elapsed.

(5) In subsection (4) above—

(a) "hospital order patient" means a patient who is subject to a hospital order, excluding a patient of a kind mentioned in paragraph (a) or (b) of subsection (2) above;

(b) "the initial detention period", in relation to a hospital order patient, means the period of six months beginning with the date of the hospital order; and

(c) "the relevant application period" means the relevant period mentioned in paragraph (ca) or (cb), as the case may be, of section 66(2) above."

21 (1) Section 72 (powers of tribunals) is amended as follows.

(2) In subsection (1)—

(a) after "this Act" insert "or is a community patient", and

(b) after paragraph (b) insert—

"(c) the tribunal shall direct the discharge of a community patient if they are not satisfied—

(i) that he is then suffering from mental disorder or mental disorder of a nature or degree which makes it appropriate for him to receive medical treatment; or

(ii) that it is necessary for his health or safety or for the protection of other persons that he should receive such treatment; or

(iii) that it is necessary that the responsible clinician should be able to exercise the power under section 17E(1) above to recall the patient to hospital; or

(iv) that appropriate medical treatment is available for him; or

(v) in the case of an application by virtue of paragraph (g) of section 66(1) above, that the patient, if discharged, would be likely to act in a manner dangerous to other persons or to himself."

(3) After subsection (1) insert—

"(1A) In determining whether the criterion in subsection (1)(c)(iii) above is met, the tribunal shall, in particular, consider, having regard to the patient's history of mental disorder and any other relevant factors, what risk there would be of a deterioration of the patient's condition if he were to continue not to be detained in a hospital (as a result, for example, of his refusing or neglecting to receive the medical treatment he requires for his mental disorder)."

(4) For subsection (3A) substitute—

"(3A) Subsection (1) above does not require a tribunal to direct the discharge of a patient just because they think it might be appropriate for the patient to be discharged (subject to the possibility of recall) under a community treatment order; and a tribunal—

(a) may recommend that the responsible clinician consider whether to make a community treatment order; and

(b) may (but need not) further consider the patient's case if the responsible clinician does not make an order."

22 In section 76 (visiting and examination of patients), in subsection (1), after "this Act" insert "or a community patient,".

23 In section 77 (general provisions concerning tribunal applications), in subsection (3) for the words from "to the tribunal" to the end substitute—

"(a) in the case of a patient who is liable to be detained in a hospital, to the tribunal for the area in which that hospital is situated;

(b) in the case of a community patient, to the tribunal for the area in which the responsible hospital is situated;

(c) in the case of a patient subject to guardianship, to the tribunal for the area in which the patient is residing."

After-care services

24 In section 117 (after-care), in subsection (2) for the words from "patient who is subject" to the end substitute "community patient while he remains such a patient."

Code of practice

25 In section 118 (code of practice), in subsection (1)(a) for "after-care under supervision" substitute "community patients".

General protection of detained patients

26 (1) Section 120 (general protection of detained patients) is amended as follows.

(2) In subsection (1)—

(a) after "liable to be detained under this Act" insert "or to community patients",

(b) in paragraph (a) after "registered establishments" insert "and community patients in hospitals and establishments of any description and (if access is granted) other places", and

(c) in paragraph (b)—

(i) in sub-paragraph (i), after "this Act in" insert ", or recalled under section 17E above to,", and

(ii) in sub-paragraph (ii), after "detained" insert "or is or has been a community patient".

(3) In subsection (4)—

(a) in paragraph (a), for "registered establishment" substitute "hospital or establishment of any description", and

(b) in paragraph (b), for "in a registered establishment" substitute "under this Act or who is or has been a community patient".

(4) After subsection (7) insert—

"(8) In this section, "establishment of any description" has the same meaning as in section 119 above."

27 In section 121 (Mental Health Act Commission), in subsection (4), for the words from "not liable" to the end substitute "neither liable to be detained under this Act nor community patients".

Offences

28 In section 128 (assisting patients to absent themselves without leave, etc), in subsection (1) after "under this Act" insert "or is a community patient".

Duty to give information

29 In section 132 (duty of managers of hospitals to give information to detained patients), in subsection (2) for "nursing home" substitute "establishment".

30 After section 132 insert—

"132A Duty of managers of hospitals to give information to community patients

"132A Duty of managers of hospitals to give information to community patients

(1) The managers of the responsible hospital shall take such steps as are practicable to ensure that a community patient understands—

(a) the effect of the provisions of this Act applying to community patients; and

(b) what rights of applying to a Mental Health Review Tribunal are available to him in that capacity;

and those steps shall be taken as soon as practicable after the patient becomes a community patient.

(2) The steps to be taken under subsection (1) above shall include giving the requisite information both orally and in writing.

(3) The managers of the responsible hospital shall, except where the community patient otherwise requests, take such steps as are practicable to furnish the person (if any) appearing to them to be his nearest relative with a copy of any information given to him in writing under subsection (1) above; and those steps shall be taken when the information is given to the patient or within a reasonable time thereafter."

31 In section 133 (duty of managers of hospitals to inform nearest relatives of discharge), after subsection (1) insert—

"(1A) The reference in subsection (1) above to a patient who is to be discharged includes a patient who is to be discharged from hospital under section 17A above.

(1B) Subsection (1) above shall also apply in a case where a community patient is discharged under section 23 or 72 above (otherwise than by virtue of an order for discharge made by his nearest relative), but with the reference in that subsection to the managers of the hospital or registered establishment being read as a reference to the managers of the responsible hospital."

Retaking of patients escaping from custody

32 In section 138 (retaking of patients escaping from custody), in subsection (1)(b) after "under this Act," insert "or a community patient who was recalled to hospital under section 17E above,".

Members of Parliament suffering from mental disorder

33 In section 141 (Members of Parliament suffering from mental disorder), after subsection (6B) (inserted by Schedule 1 to this Act) insert—

"(6C) References in this section to a member who is authorised to be detained shall not include a member who is a community patient (whether or not he is recalled to hospital under section 17E above)."

Interpretation

34 (1) Section 145 (interpretation) is amended as follows.

(2) In subsection (1), in the definition of "absent without leave", after "related expressions" insert "(including expressions relating to a patient's liability to be returned to a hospital or other place)".

(3) In that subsection, at the appropriate places insert—

"“community patient” has the meaning given in section 17A above;"

"“community treatment order” and “the community treatment order” have the meanings given in section 17A above;"

"“the community treatment period” has the meaning given in section 20A above;"

"""the responsible hospital" has the meaning given in section 17A above;".

(4) In subsection (3), after "guardianship" insert "or a community patient".

Extent

35 (1) In section 146 (application to Scotland), omit the words from "128" to "guardianship)".

(2) This paragraph does not extend to Scotland.

Application of certain provisions to patients concerned in criminal proceedings

36 (1) In Schedule 1 (application of certain provisions to patients subject to hospital and guardianship orders), Part 1 (patients not subject to special restrictions) is amended as follows.

(2) In paragraph 1, after "17" insert "to 17C, 17E, 17F, 20A".

(3) In paragraph 2—

(a) for "18, 19, 20" substitute "17D, 17G, 18 to 20, 20B", and

(b) for "paragraphs 3" substitute "paragraphs 2A".

(4) After paragraph 2 insert—

"2A In section 17D(2)(a) for the reference to section 6(2) above there shall be substituted a reference to section 40(1)(b) below.

2B In section 17G—

(a) in subsection (2) for the reference to section 6(2) above there shall be substituted a reference to section 40(1)(b) below;

(b) in subsection (4) for paragraphs (a) and (b) there shall be substituted the words "the order or direction under Part 3 of this Act in respect of him were an order or direction for his admission or removal to that other hospital"; and

(c) in subsection (5) for the words from "the patient" to the end there shall be substituted the words "the date of the relevant order or direction under Part 3 of this Act were the date on which the community treatment order is revoked"."

(5) After paragraph 5 insert—

"5A In section 19A(2), paragraph (b) shall be omitted."

(6) After paragraph 6 insert—

"6A In section 20B(1), for the reference to the application for admission for treatment there shall be substituted a reference to the order or direction under Part 3 of this Act by virtue of which the patient is liable to be detained."

(7) In paragraph 8(b), for "and (b)" substitute "to (c)".

37 (1) Part 2 of that Schedule (patients subject to special restrictions) is amended as follows.

(2) In paragraph 2, for "17 to 19" substitute "17, 18, 19".

(3) For paragraph 6 substitute—

"6 In section 22, subsections (1) and (5) shall not apply."

SCHEDULE 4

Section 32

SUPERVISED COMMUNITY TREATMENT: AMENDMENTS TO OTHER ACTS

Administration of Justice Act 1960

1 After section 5 of the Administration of Justice Act 1960 (c. 65) insert—

"5A Power to order continuation of community treatment order

"5A Power to order continuation of community treatment order

(1) Where the defendant in any proceedings from which an appeal lies under section 1 of this Act would, but for the decision of the court below, be liable to recall, and immediately after that decision the prosecutor is granted, or gives notice that he intends to apply for, leave to appeal, the court may make an order under this section.

(2) For the purposes of this section, a person is liable to recall if he is subject to a community treatment order (within the meaning of the Mental Health Act 1983) and, when that order was made, he was liable to be detained in pursuance of an order or direction under Part 3 of that Act.

(3) An order under this section is an order providing for the continuation of the community treatment order and the order or direction under Part 3 of that Act so long as any appeal under section 1 of this Act is pending.

(4) Where the court makes an order under this section, the provisions of the Mental Health Act 1983 with respect to persons liable to recall (including provisions as to the extension of the community treatment period, the removal or discharge of community patients, the revocation of community treatment orders and the re-detention of patients following revocation) shall apply accordingly.

(5) An order under this section shall (unless the appeal has previously been disposed of) cease to have effect at the expiration of the period for which the defendant would, but for the decision of the court below, have been—

(a) liable to recall; or

(b) where the community treatment order is revoked, liable to be detained in pursuance of the order or direction under Part 3 of the Mental Health Act 1983.

(6) Where the court below has power to make an order under this section, and either no such order is made or the defendant is discharged by virtue of subsection (4) or (5) of this section before the appeal is disposed of, the defendant shall not be liable to be again detained as the result of the decision of the Supreme Court on the appeal."

Criminal Appeal Act 1968

2 (1) The Criminal Appeal Act 1968 (c. 19) is amended as follows.

(2) In section 8 (supplementary provisions as to retrial), after subsection (3A) insert—

"(3B) If the person ordered to be retried—

(a) was liable to be detained in pursuance of an order or direction under Part 3 of the Mental Health Act 1983;

(b) was then made subject to a community treatment order (within the meaning of that Act); and

(c) was subject to that community treatment order immediately before the determination of his appeal,

the order or direction under Part 3 of that Act and the community treatment order shall continue in force pending the retrial as if the appeal had not been allowed, and any order made by the Court of Appeal under this section for his release on bail shall have effect subject to the community treatment order."

(3) After section 37 insert—

"37A Continuation of community treatment order on appeal by the Crown

"37A Continuation of community treatment order on appeal by the Crown

(1) The following provisions apply where, immediately after a decision of the Court of Appeal from which an appeal lies to the Supreme Court, the prosecutor is granted, or gives notice that he intends to apply for, leave to appeal.

(2) If, but for the decision of the Court of Appeal, the defendant would be liable to recall, the Court of Appeal may make an order under this section.

(3) For the purposes of this section, a person is liable to recall if he is subject to a community treatment order (within the meaning of the Mental Health Act 1983) and, when that order was made, he was liable to be detained in pursuance of an order or direction under Part 3 of that Act.

(4) An order under this section is an order providing for the continuation of the community treatment order and the order or direction under Part 3 of that Act so long as an appeal to the Supreme Court is pending.

(5) Where an order is made under this section the provisions of the Mental Health Act 1983 with respect to persons liable to recall (including provisions as to the extension of the community treatment period, the removal or discharge of community patients, the revocation of community treatment orders and the re-detention of patients following revocation) shall apply accordingly.

(6) An order under this section shall (unless the appeal has previously been disposed of) cease to have effect at the expiration of the period for which the defendant would, but for the decision of the Court of Appeal, have been—

(a) liable to recall; or

(b) where the community treatment order is revoked, liable to be detained in pursuance of the order or direction under Part 3 of the Mental Health Act 1983.

(7) Where the Court of Appeal have power to make an order under this section, and either no such order is made or the defendant is discharged, by virtue of subsection (5) or (6) of this section, before the appeal is disposed of, the defendant shall not be liable to be again detained as the result of the decision of the Supreme Court on the appeal."

Courts-Martial (Appeals) Act 1968

3 (1) The Courts-Martial (Appeals) Act 1968 (c. 20) is amended as follows.

(2) In section 20 (implementation of authority for retrial etc), after subsection (4) insert—

"(4A) Where retrial is authorised in the case of a person who—

(a) was liable to be detained in pursuance of an order or direction under Part 3 of the Mental Health Act 1983;

(b) was then made subject to a community treatment order (within the meaning of that Act); and

(c) was subject to that community treatment order immediately before the date of the authorisation,

the order or direction under Part 3 of that Act and the community treatment order shall continue in force until the relevant time (as defined in subsection (3A)) as if his conviction had not been quashed.

(4B) An order under subsection (1E)(a) is of no effect in relation to a person for so long as he is subject to a community treatment order."

(3) In section 43 (detention of accused), after subsection (3) insert—

"(3A) The relevant provisions of the Mental Health Act 1983 with respect to community treatment orders (within the meaning of that Act) shall also apply for the purposes of subsection (3)."

(4) After that section insert—

"43A Continuation of community treatment order

"43A Continuation of community treatment order

(1) The Appeal Court may make an order under this section where—

(a) but for the decision of the Appeal Court, the accused would be liable to recall; and

(b) immediately after that decision, the Director of Service Prosecutions is granted leave to appeal or gives notice that he intends to apply for leave to appeal.

(2) For the purposes of this section, a person is liable to recall if he is subject to a community treatment order (within the meaning of the Mental Health Act 1983) and, when that order was made, he was liable to be detained in pursuance of an order or direction under Part 3 of that Act.

(3) An order under this section is an order providing for the continuation of the community treatment order and the order or direction under Part 3 of that Act so long as any appeal to the Supreme Court is pending.

(4) Where the Appeal Court makes an order under this section, the relevant provisions of the Mental Health Act 1983 with respect to persons liable to recall (including provisions as to the extension of the community treatment period, the removal or discharge of community patients, the revocation of community treatment orders and the re-detention of patients following revocation) shall apply accordingly.

(5) An order under this section shall (unless the appeal has been previously disposed of) cease to have effect at the end of the period for which the accused would, but for the decision of the Appeal Court, have been—

(a) liable to recall; or

(b) where the community treatment order is revoked, liable to be detained in pursuance of the order or direction under Part 3 of the Mental Health Act 1983.

(6) Where the Appeal Court has power to make an order under this section and either no such order is made or the accused is discharged by virtue of subsection (4) or (5) above before the appeal is disposed of, the accused shall not be liable to be again detained as a result of the decision of the Supreme Court on the appeal."

Juries Act 1974

4 In Schedule 1 to the Juries Act 1974 (c. 23) (mentally disordered persons and persons disqualified from serving), at the end of paragraph 2 insert "or subject to a community treatment order under section 17A of that Act".

SCHEDULE 5

Section 39

CROSS-BORDER ARRANGEMENTS

PART 1

AMENDMENTS TO PART 6 OF 1983 ACT

Introduction

1 Part 6 of the 1983 Act is amended as set out in this Part of this Schedule.

Transfer of patients: Scotland

2 In section 80 (removal of patients to Scotland) (the cross-heading immediately above which becomes "Removal to and from Scotland"), in subsection (1), omit the words "or subject to guardianship" and the words "or, as the case may be, for receiving him into guardianship".

3 (1) After that section insert—

"80ZA Transfer of responsibility for community patients to Scotland

"80ZA Transfer of responsibility for community patients to Scotland

(1) If it appears to the appropriate national authority, in the case of a community patient, that the conditions mentioned in subsection (2) below are met, the authority may authorise the transfer of responsibility for him to Scotland.

(2) The conditions are—

(a) a transfer under this section is in the patient's interests; and

(b) arrangements have been made for dealing with him under enactments in force in Scotland corresponding or similar to those relating to community patients in this Act.

(3) The appropriate national authority may not act under subsection (1) above while the patient is recalled to hospital under section 17E above.

(4) In this section, "the appropriate national authority" means—

(a) in relation to a community patient in respect of whom the responsible hospital is in England, the Secretary of State;

(b) in relation to a community patient in respect of whom the responsible hospital is in Wales, the Welsh Ministers."

(2) This paragraph does not extend to Scotland.

4 (1) After section 80A (the title to which becomes "Transfer of responsibility for conditionally discharged patients to Scotland") insert—

"80B Removal of detained patients from Scotland

"80B Removal of detained patients from Scotland

(1) This section applies to a patient if—

(a) he is removed to England and Wales under regulations made under section 290(1)(a) of the Mental Health (Care and Treatment) (Scotland) Act 2003 ("the 2003 Act");

(b) immediately before his removal, his detention in hospital was authorised by virtue of that Act or the Criminal Procedure (Scotland) Act 1995; and

(c) on his removal, he is admitted to a hospital in England or Wales.

(2) He shall be treated as if, on the date of his admission to the hospital, he had been so admitted in pursuance of an application made, or an order or direction made or given, on that date under the enactment in force in England and Wales which most closely corresponds to the enactment by virtue of which his detention in hospital was authorised immediately before his removal.

(3) If, immediately before his removal, he was subject to a measure under any enactment in force in Scotland restricting his discharge, he shall be treated as if he were subject to an order or direction under the enactment in force in England and Wales which most closely corresponds to that enactment.

(4) If, immediately before his removal, the patient was liable to be detained under the 2003 Act by virtue of a transfer for treatment direction, given while he was serving a sentence of imprisonment (within the meaning of section 136(9) of that Act) imposed by a court in Scotland, he shall be treated as if the sentence had been imposed by a court in England and Wales.

(5) If, immediately before his removal, the patient was subject to a hospital direction or transfer for treatment direction, the restriction direction to which he is subject by virtue of subsection (3) above shall expire on the date on which that hospital direction or transfer for treatment direction (as the case may be) would have expired if he had not been so removed.

(6) If, immediately before his removal, the patient was liable to be detained under the 2003 Act by virtue of a hospital direction, he shall be treated as if any sentence of imprisonment passed at the time when that hospital direction was made had been imposed by a court in England and Wales.

(7) Any directions given by the Scottish Ministers under regulations made under section 290 of the 2003 Act as to the removal of a patient to which this section applies shall have effect as if they were given under this Act.

(8) Subsection (8) of section 80 above applies to a reference in this section as it applies to one in that section.

(9) In this section—

"hospital direction" means a direction made under section 59A of the Criminal Procedure (Scotland) Act 1995; and

"transfer for treatment direction" has the meaning given by section 136 of the 2003 Act.

80C Removal of patients subject to compulsion in the community from Scotland

80C Removal of patients subject to compulsion in the community from Scotland

(1) This section applies to a patient if—

(a) he is subject to an enactment in force in Scotland by virtue of which regulations under section 289(1) of the Mental Health (Care and Treatment) (Scotland) Act 2003 apply to him; and

(b) he is removed to England and Wales under those regulations.

(2) He shall be treated as if on the date of his arrival at the place where he is to reside in England or Wales—

(a) he had been admitted to a hospital in England or Wales in pursuance of an application or order made on that date under the corresponding enactment; and

(b) a community treatment order had then been made discharging him from the hospital.

(3) For these purposes—

(a) if the enactment to which the patient was subject in Scotland was an enactment contained in the Mental Health (Care and Treatment)

(Scotland) Act 2003, the corresponding enactment is section 3 of this Act;

(b) if the enactment to which he was subject in Scotland was an enactment contained in the Criminal Procedure (Scotland) Act 1995, the corresponding enactment is section 37 of this Act.

(4) "The responsible hospital", in the case of a patient in respect of whom a community treatment order is in force by virtue of subsection (2) above, means the hospital to which he is treated as having been admitted by virtue of that subsection, subject to section 19A above.

(5) As soon as practicable after the patient's arrival at the place where he is to reside in England or Wales, the responsible clinician shall specify the conditions to which he is to be subject for the purposes of section 17B(1) above, and the conditions shall be deemed to be specified in the community treatment order.

(6) But the responsible clinician may only specify conditions under subsection (5) above which an approved mental health professional agrees should be specified.

80D Transfer of conditionally discharged patients from Scotland

80D Transfer of conditionally discharged patients from Scotland

(1) This section applies to a patient who is subject to—

(a) a restriction order under section 59 of the Criminal Procedure (Scotland) Act 1995; and

(b) a conditional discharge under section 193(7) of the Mental Health (Care and Treatment) (Scotland) Act 2003 ("the 2003 Act").

(2) A transfer of the patient to England and Wales under regulations made under section 290 of the 2003 Act shall have effect only if the Secretary of State has consented to the transfer.

(3) If a transfer under those regulations has effect, the patient shall be treated as if—

(a) on the date of the transfer he had been conditionally discharged under section 42 or 73 above; and

(b) he were subject to a hospital order under section 37 above and a restriction order under section 41 above.

(4) If the restriction order to which the patient was subject immediately before the transfer was of limited duration, the restriction order to which he is subject by virtue of subsection (3) above shall expire on the date on which the first-mentioned order would have expired if the transfer had not been made."

(2) This paragraph does not extend to Scotland.

Transfer of patients: Northern Ireland

5 In section 81 (removal of patients to Northern Ireland), in subsection (2), for the words from "where he is" to "the corresponding enactment" substitute "where he is subject to a hospital order and a restriction order or a transfer direction and a

restriction direction under any enactment in this Act, as if he were subject to a hospital order and a restriction order or a transfer direction and a restriction direction under the corresponding enactment".

6 After that section insert—

"81ZA Removal of community patients to Northern Ireland

"81ZA Removal of community patients to Northern Ireland

(1) Section 81 above shall apply in the case of a community patient as it applies in the case of a patient who is for the time being liable to be detained under this Act, as if the community patient were so liable.

(2) Any reference in that section to the application, order or direction by virtue of which a patient is liable to be detained under this Act shall be construed, for these purposes, as a reference to the application, order or direction under this Act in respect of the patient."

7 (1) Section 81A (transfer of responsibility for patients to Northern Ireland) is amended as follows.

(2) For subsection (1)(a) substitute—

"(a) is subject to a hospital order under section 37 above and a restriction order under section 41 above or to a transfer direction under section 47 above and a restriction direction under section 49 above;"

(3) In subsection (2)(b), for "a restriction order or restriction direction" substitute "a hospital order and a restriction order, or to a transfer direction and a restriction direction,".

8 In section 82 (removal to England and Wales of patients from Northern Ireland), in subsection (2), for the words from "where he is" to "the corresponding enactment" substitute "where he is subject to a hospital order and a restriction order or a transfer direction and a restriction direction under any enactment in that Order, as if he were subject to a hospital order and a restriction order or a transfer direction and a restriction direction under the corresponding enactment".

9 In section 82A (the title to which becomes "Transfer of responsibility for conditionally discharged patients to England and Wales from Northern Ireland), for subsection (2)(b) substitute—

"(b) as if he were subject to a hospital order under section 37 above and a restriction order under section 41 above or to a transfer direction under section 47 above and a restriction direction under section 49 above."

Transfer of patients: Channel Islands and Isle of Man

10 Before section 83A (the title to which becomes "Transfer of responsibility for conditionally discharged patients to Channel Islands or Isle of Man") insert—

"83ZA Removal or transfer of community patients to Channel Islands or Isle of Man

"83ZA Removal or transfer of community patients to Channel Islands or Isle of Man

(1) Section 83 above shall apply in the case of a community patient as it applies in the case of a patient who is for the time being liable to be detained under this Act, as if the community patient were so liable.

(2) But if there are in force in any of the Channel Islands or the Isle of Man enactments ("relevant enactments") corresponding or similar to those relating to community patients in this Act—

(a) subsection (1) above shall not apply as regards that island; and

(b) subsections (3) to (6) below shall apply instead.

(3) If it appears to the appropriate national authority, in the case of a community patient, that the conditions mentioned in subsection (4) below are met, the authority may authorise the transfer of responsibility for him to the island in question.

(4) The conditions are—

(a) a transfer under subsection (3) above is in the patient's interests; and

(b) arrangements have been made for dealing with him under the relevant enactments.

(5) But the authority may not act under subsection (3) above while the patient is recalled to hospital under section 17E above.

(6) In this section, "the appropriate national authority" means—

(a) in relation to a community patient in respect of whom the responsible hospital is in England, the Secretary of State;

(b) in relation to a community patient in respect of whom the responsible hospital is in Wales, the Welsh Ministers."

11 In section 85 (patients removed from Channel Islands or Isle of Man), in subsection (2), for "to a restriction order or restriction direction" substitute "to a hospital order and a restriction order or to a hospital direction and a limitation direction or to a transfer direction and a restriction direction".

12 Before section 85A (the title to which becomes "Responsibility for conditionally discharged patients transferred from Channel Islands or Isle of Man") insert—

"85ZA Responsibility for community patients transferred from Channel Islands or Isle of Man

"85ZA Responsibility for community patients transferred from Channel Islands or Isle of Man

(1) This section shall have effect if there are in force in any of the Channel Islands or the Isle of Man enactments ("relevant enactments") corresponding or similar to those relating to community patients in this Act.

(2) If responsibility for a patient is transferred to England and Wales under a provision corresponding to section 83ZA(3) above, he shall be treated as if on the date of his arrival at the place where he is to reside in England or Wales—

(a) he had been admitted to the hospital in pursuance of an application made, or an order or direction made or given, on that date under the enactment in force in England and Wales which most closely corresponds to the relevant enactments; and

(b) a community treatment order had then been made discharging him from the hospital.

(3) "The responsible hospital", in his case, means the hospital to which he is treated as having been admitted by virtue of subsection (2) above, subject to section 19A above.

(4) As soon as practicable after the patient's arrival at the place where he is to reside in England or Wales, the responsible clinician shall specify the conditions to which he is to be subject for the purposes of section 17B(1) above, and the conditions shall be deemed to be specified in the community treatment order.

(5) But the responsible clinician may only specify conditions under subsection (4) above which an approved mental health professional agrees should be specified."

13 (1) Section 85A is amended as follows.

(2) For subsection (2)(b) substitute—

"(b) as if he were subject to a hospital order under section 37 above and a restriction order under section 41 above, or to a hospital direction and a limitation direction under section 45A above, or to a transfer direction under section 47 above and a restriction direction under section 49 above."

(3) In subsection (3) after "restriction order" insert ", limitation direction".

Patients absent from hospitals in England and Wales

14 (1) Section 88 (patients absent from hospitals in England and Wales) is amended as follows.

(2) In subsection (1) for the words from "any other part" to the end substitute "Northern Ireland".

(3) For subsection (2) substitute—

"(2) For the purposes of the enactments referred to in subsection (1) above in their application by virtue of this section, the expression "constable" includes an officer or constable of the Police Service of Northern Ireland."

(4) In subsection (3) omit the following—

(a) the words "to Scotland or Northern Ireland",

(b) paragraph (a), and

(c) in paragraph (b), the words "in Northern Ireland,".

Regulations for purposes of Part 6

15 In section 90 (regulations for purposes of Part 6), for the words from "and to regulations" to the end substitute ", so far as this Part of this Act applies to patients removed to England and Wales or for whom responsibility is transferred to England and Wales."

General provisions as to patients removed from England and Wales

16 In section 91 (general provisions as to patients removed from England and Wales), after subsection (2) insert—

"(2A) Where responsibility for a community patient is transferred to a jurisdiction outside England and Wales (or such a patient is removed outside England and Wales) in pursuance of arrangements under this Part of this Act, the application, order or direction mentioned in subsection (1) above in force in respect of him shall cease to have effect on the date on which responsibility is so transferred (or he is so removed) in pursuance of those arrangements."

Interpretation

17 In section 92 (interpretation of Part 6), after subsection (1) insert—

"(1A) References in this Part of this Act to the responsible clinician shall be construed as references to the responsible clinician within the meaning of Part 2 of this Act."

PART 2

RELATED AMENDMENTS

The 1983 Act

18 In section 69 of the 1983 Act (applications to tribunals concerning patients subject to hospital and guardianship orders), in subsection (2)(a)—

(a) after "hospital order" insert ", hospital direction", and
(b) for the words from ", 82(2) or" to the end substitute "or section 80B(2), 82(2) or 85(2) below."

19 (1) Section 79 of that Act (interpretation of Part 5) is amended as follows.

(2) In subsection (1), for paragraph (c) substitute—

"(c) is treated as subject to a hospital order and a restriction order, or to a hospital direction and a limitation direction, or to a transfer direction and a restriction direction, by virtue of any provision of Part 6 of this Act (except section 80D(3), 82A(2) or 85A(2) below),".

(3) In subsection (5)—

(a) after "the relevant hospital order," insert "the relevant hospital direction,",
(b) after "the restriction order" insert ", the limitation direction",
(c) after "the hospital order," insert "hospital direction,", and
(d) after "restriction order," insert "limitation direction,".

(4) After that subsection insert—

"(5A) Section 75 above shall, subject to the modifications in subsection (5C) below, have effect in relation to a qualifying patient as it has effect in relation to a restricted patient who is conditionally discharged under section 42(2), 73 or 74 above.

(5B) A patient is a qualifying patient if he is treated by virtue of section 80D(3), 82A(2) or 85A(2) below as if he had been conditionally discharged and were subject to a hospital order and a restriction order, or to a hospital direction and a limitation direction, or to a transfer direction and a restriction direction.

(5C) The modifications mentioned in subsection (5A) above are—

(a) references to the relevant hospital order, hospital direction or transfer direction, or to the restriction order, limitation direction or restriction direction to which the patient is subject, shall be construed as references to the hospital order, hospital direction or transfer direction, or restriction order, limitation direction or restriction direction, to which the patient is treated as subject by virtue of section 80D(3), 82A(2) or 85A(2) below; and

(b) the reference to the date on which the patient was conditionally discharged shall be construed as a reference to the date on which he was treated as conditionally discharged by virtue of a provision mentioned in paragraph (a) above."

20 (1) In section 146 (application to Scotland), omit the words from "88" to "138)".

(2) This paragraph does not extend to Scotland.

Mental Health (Care and Treatment) (Scotland) Act 2003 (Consequential Provisions) Order 2005 (S.I. 2005/2078)

21 (1) The Mental Health (Care and Treatment) (Scotland) Act 2003 (Consequential Provisions) Order 2005 is amended as follows.

(2) Omit the following provisions—

(a) article 1(5),

(b) article 2, and

(c) article 3.

(3) In article 8 (the title to which becomes "Patients absent from hospitals or other places in Scotland"), in paragraph (1)(b), for "290" substitute "289, 290, 309, 309A".

(4) In article 12(2), for "2 to 11" substitute "4 to 11".

SCHEDULE 6

Section 48

VICTIMS' RIGHTS

Introduction

1 Chapter 2 of Part 3 of the Domestic Violence, Crime and Victims Act 2004 (c. 28) (provision of information to victims of restricted patients under the 1983 Act, etc.) is amended as set out in this Schedule.

Hospital orders (with or without restriction orders)

2 (1) Section 36 (victims' rights: preliminary) is amended as follows.

(2) In subsection (3), for "with a restriction order" substitute ", whether with or without a restriction order,".

(3) In subsection (5)—

(a) in paragraph (a), after "discharge from hospital" insert "while a restriction order is in force in respect of him", and

(b) after paragraph (b) insert ";

(c) what conditions he should be subject to in the event of his discharge from hospital under a community treatment order".

3 After section 36 insert—

"36A Supplemental provision for case where no restriction order made

"36A Supplemental provision for case where no restriction order made

(1) This section applies if, in a case where section 36 applies, the hospital order in respect of the patient was made without a restriction order.

(2) Subsection (3) applies if a person who appears to the local probation board mentioned in section 36(4) to be the victim of the offence or to act for the victim of the offence, when his wishes are ascertained under section 36(4), expresses a wish—

(a) to make representations about a matter specified in section 36(5), or

(b) to receive the information specified in section 36(6).

(3) The local probation board must—

(a) notify the managers of the hospital in which the patient is detained of that person's wish and of that person's name and address, and

(b) notify that person of the name and address of the hospital.

(4) Subsection (5) applies if a person who appears to the local probation board mentioned in section 36(4) to be the victim of the offence or to act for the victim of the offence, subsequently to his wishes being ascertained under section 36(4), expresses a wish to do something specified in subsection (2) (a) or (b).

(5) The local probation board mentioned in section 36(4) must take all reasonable steps—

(a) to ascertain whether the hospital order made in respect of the patient continues in force and whether a community treatment order is in force in respect of him, and

(b) if the board ascertains that the hospital order does continue in force—

(i) to notify the managers of the relevant hospital of that person's wish, and

(ii) to notify that person of the name and address of the hospital.

(6) The relevant hospital is—

(a) the hospital in which the patient is detained, or

(b) if a community treatment order is in force in respect of the patient, the responsible hospital."

4 In section 37 (the title to which becomes "Representations where restriction order made"), in subsection (1), for "if section 36 applies" substitute "if, in a case where section 36 applies, the hospital order in respect of the patient was made with a restriction order".

5 After section 37 insert—

"37A Representations where restriction order not made

"37A Representations where restriction order not made

(1) This section applies if, in a case where section 36 applies, the hospital order in respect of the patient was made without a restriction order.

(2) Subsection (3) applies if—

(a) a person makes representations about a matter specified in section 36(5) to the managers of the relevant hospital, and

(b) it appears to the managers that the person is the victim of the offence or acts for the victim of the offence.

(3) The managers must forward the representations to the persons responsible for determining the matter.

(4) The responsible clinician must inform the managers of the relevant hospital if he is considering making—

(a) an order for discharge in respect of the patient under section 23(2) of the Mental Health Act 1983,

(b) a community treatment order in respect of the patient, or

(c) an order under section 17B(4) of the Mental Health Act 1983 to vary the conditions specified in a community treatment order in force in respect of the patient.

(5) Any person who has the power to make an order for discharge in respect of the patient under section 23(3) of the Mental Health Act 1983 must inform the managers of the relevant hospital if he is considering making that order.

(6) A Mental Health Review Tribunal must inform the managers of the relevant hospital if—

(a) an application is made to the tribunal under section 66 or 69 of the Mental Health Act 1983, or

(b) the patient's case is referred to the tribunal under section 67 of that Act.

(7) Subsection (8) applies if—

(a) the managers of the relevant hospital receive information under subsection (4), (5) or (6), and

(b) a person who appears to the managers to be the victim of the offence or to act for the victim of the offence—

(i) when his wishes were ascertained under section 36(4), expressed a wish to make representations about a matter specified in section 36(5), or

(ii) has made representations about such a matter to the managers of the hospital in which the patient was, at the time in question, detained.

(8) The managers of the relevant hospital must provide the information to the person.

(9) The relevant hospital has the meaning given in section 36A(6)."

6 In section 38 (the title to which becomes "Information where restriction order made"), in subsection (1) for "if section 36 applies" substitute "if, in a case where section 36 applies, the hospital order in respect of the patient was made with a restriction order".

7 After section 38 insert —

"38A Information where restriction order not made

"38A Information where restriction order not made

(1) This section applies if, in a case where section 36 applies, the hospital order in respect of the patient was made without a restriction order.

(2) The responsible clinician must inform the managers of the relevant hospital—

(a) whether he is to make an order for discharge in respect of the patient under section 23(2) of the Mental Health Act 1983;

(b) whether he is to make a community treatment order in respect of the patient;

(c) if a community treatment order is to be made in respect of the patient, what conditions are to be specified in the order;

(d) if a community treatment order is in force in respect of the patient, of any variation to be made under section 17B(4) of the Mental Health Act 1983 of the conditions specified in the order;

(e) if a community treatment order in respect of the patient is to cease to be in force, of the date on which it is to cease to be in force;

(f) if, following the examination of the patient under section 20 of the Mental Health Act 1983, it does not appear to the responsible clinician that the conditions set out in subsection (4) of that section are satisfied, of the date on which the authority for the patient's detention is to expire.

(3) Any person who has the power to make an order for discharge in respect of the patient under section 23(3) of the Mental Health Act 1983 must inform the managers of the relevant hospital if he is to make that order.

(4) Subsection (5) applies if—

(a) an application is made to a Mental Health Review Tribunal under section 66 or 69 of the Mental Health Act 1983,

(b) the patient's case is referred to a Mental Health Review Tribunal under section 67 of that Act, or

(c) the managers of the relevant hospital refer the patient's case to a Mental Health Review Tribunal under section 68 of that Act.

(5) The tribunal must inform the managers of the relevant hospital if it directs that the patient is to be discharged.

(6) Subsection (7) applies if a person who appears to the managers of the relevant hospital to be the victim of the offence or to act for the victim of the offence—

(a) when his wishes were ascertained under section 36(4), expressed a wish to receive the information specified in section 36(6), or

(b) has subsequently informed the managers of the relevant hospital that he wishes to receive that information.

(7) The managers of the relevant hospital order must take all reasonable steps—

(a) to inform that person whether the patient is to be discharged under section 23 or 72 of the Mental Health Act 1983;

(b) to inform that person whether a community treatment order is to be made in respect of the patient;

(c) if a community treatment order is to be made in respect of the patient and is to specify conditions which relate to contact with the victim or his family, to provide that person with details of those conditions;

(d) if a community treatment order is in force in respect of the patient and the conditions specified in the order are to be varied under section 17B(4) of the Mental Health Act 1983, to provide that person with details of any variation which relates to contact with the victim or his family;

(e) if a community treatment order in respect of the patient is to cease to be in force, to inform that person of the date on which it is to cease to be in force;

(f) if, following the examination of the patient under section 20 of the Mental Health Act 1983, the authority for the patient's detention is not to be renewed, to inform that person of the date on which the authority is to expire;

(g) to provide that person with such other information as the managers of the relevant hospital consider appropriate in all the circumstances of the case.

(8) The relevant hospital has the meaning given by section 36A(6).

38B Removal of restriction

38B Removal of restriction

(1) This section applies if, in a case where section 36 applies—

- (a) the hospital order in respect of the patient was made with a restriction order, and
- (b) the restriction order ceases to have effect while the hospital order continues in force.

(2) Subsection (3) applies if a person who appears to the relevant local probation board to be the victim of the offence or to act for the victim of the offence—

- (a) when his wishes were ascertained under section 36(4), expressed a wish to make representations about a matter specified in section 36(5) or to receive the information specified in section 36(6), or
- (b) has subsequently informed the relevant local probation board that he wishes to make representations about such a matter or to receive that information.

(3) The relevant local probation board must take all reasonable steps—

- (a) to notify the managers of the relevant hospital of an address at which that person may be contacted;
- (b) to notify that person of the name and address of the hospital.

(4) While the hospital order continues in force, the patient is to be regarded as a patient in respect of whom a hospital order was made without a restriction order; and sections 37A and 38A are to apply in relation to him accordingly.

(5) The relevant hospital has the meaning given in section 36A(6).

(6) The relevant local probation board has the meaning given in section 37(8)."

Hospital directions and limitation directions

8 In section 39 (victims' rights: preliminary), in subsection (3)—

- (a) in paragraph (a), after "discharge from hospital" insert "while he is subject to a limitation direction", and
- (b) after that paragraph insert—
  - "(aa) what conditions he should be subject to in the event of his discharge from hospital under a community treatment order;".

9 After section 41 insert—

"41A Removal of restriction

"41A Removal of restriction

(1) This section applies if, in a case where section 39 applies—

- (a) the limitation direction in respect of the offender ceases to be in force, and

(b) he is treated for the purposes of the Mental Health Act 1983 as a patient in respect of whom a hospital order has effect.

(2) Subsection (3) applies if a person who appears to the relevant local probation board to be the victim of the offence or to act for the victim of the offence—

(a) when his wishes were ascertained under section 39(2), expressed a wish to make representations about a matter specified in section 39(3) or to receive the information specified in section 39(4), or

(b) has subsequently informed the relevant local probation board that he wishes to make representations about such a matter or to receive that information.

(3) The relevant local probation board must take all reasonable steps—

(a) to notify the managers of the relevant hospital of an address at which that person may be contacted;

(b) to notify that person of the address of the hospital.

(4) The offender is to be regarded as a patient in respect of whom a hospital order was made without a restriction order; and sections 37A and 38A are to apply in relation to him accordingly.

(5) The relevant hospital has the meaning given in section 36A(6).

(6) The relevant local probation board has the meaning given in section 40(8)."

Transfer directions (with or without restriction directions)

10 (1) Section 42 (victims' rights: preliminary) is amended as follows.

(2) In subsection (1)(c), for "and a restriction direction in respect of him" substitute "in respect of the offender (whether or not he also gives a restriction direction in respect of the offender)".

(3) In subsection (3)—

(a) in paragraph (a), after "discharge from hospital" insert "at a time when a restriction direction is in force in respect of him", and

(b) after paragraph (b) insert ";

(c) what conditions he should be subject to in the event of his discharge from hospital under a community treatment order".

11 After section 42 insert—

"42A Supplemental provision for case where no restriction direction given

"42A Supplemental provision for case where no restriction direction given

(1) This section applies if, in a case where section 42 applies, the transfer direction in respect of the patient was given without a restriction direction.

(2) Subsection (3) applies if a person who appears to the local probation board mentioned in section 42(2) to be the victim of the offence or to act for the

victim of the offence, when his wishes are ascertained under section 42(2), expresses a wish—

(a) to make representations about a matter specified in section 42(3), or

(b) to receive the information specified in section 42(4).

(3) The local probation board must—

(a) notify the managers of the hospital in which the patient is detained of that person's wish and of that person's name and address, and

(b) notify that person of the name and address of the hospital.

(4) Subsection (5) applies if a person who appears to the local probation board mentioned in section 42(2) to be the victim of the offence or to act for the victim of the offence, subsequently to his wishes being ascertained under section 42(2), expressed a wish to do something specified in subsection (2)(a) or (b).

(5) The local probation board mentioned in section 42(2) must take all reasonable steps—

(a) to ascertain whether the transfer direction given in respect of the patient continues in force and whether a community treatment order is in force in respect of him, and

(b) if the board ascertains that the transfer direction does continue in force—

(i) to notify the managers of the relevant hospital of that person's wish, and

(ii) to notify that person of the name and address of the hospital.

(6) The relevant hospital has the meaning given in section 36A(6)."

12 In section 43 (the title to which becomes "Representations where restriction direction made"), in subsection (1), for "if section 42 applies" substitute "if, in a case where section 42 applies, the transfer direction in respect of the patient was given with a restriction direction".

13 After section 43 insert—

"43A Representations where restriction direction not given

"43A Representations where restriction direction not given

(1) This section applies if, in a case where section 42 applies, the transfer direction in respect of the patient was given without a restriction direction.

(2) Subsection (3) applies if—

(a) a person makes representations about a matter specified in section 42(3) to the managers of the relevant hospital, and

(b) it appears to the managers that the person is the victim of the offence or acts for the victim of the offence.

(3) The managers must forward the representations to the persons responsible for determining the matter.

(4) The responsible clinician must inform the managers of the relevant hospital if he is considering making—

(a) an order for discharge in respect of the patient under section 23(2) of the Mental Health Act 1983,

(b) a community treatment order in respect of him, or

(c) an order under section 17B(4) of the Mental Health Act 1983 to vary the conditions specified in a community treatment order in force in respect of the patient.

(5) Any person who has power to make an order for discharge in respect of the patient under section 23(3) of the Mental Health Act 1983 must inform the managers of the relevant hospital if he is considering making that order.

(6) A Mental Health Review Tribunal must inform the managers of the relevant hospital if—

(a) an application is made to the tribunal under section 66 or 69 of the Mental Health Act 1983, or

(b) the patient's case is referred to the tribunal under section 67 of that Act.

(7) Subsection (8) applies if—

(a) the managers of the relevant hospital receive information under subsection (4), (5) or (6), and

(b) a person who appears to the managers to be the victim of the offence or to act for the victim of the offence—

(i) when his wishes were ascertained under section 42(2), expressed a wish to make representations about a matter specified in section 42(3), or

(ii) has made representations about such a matter to the managers of the hospital in which the patient was, at the time in question, detained.

(8) The managers of the relevant hospital must provide the information to the person.

(9) The relevant hospital has the meaning given in section 36A(6)."

14 In section 44 (the title to which becomes "Information where restriction direction made"), in subsection (1), for "if section 42 applies" substitute "if, in a case where section 42 applies, the transfer direction in respect of the patient was given with a restriction direction".

15 After section 44 insert —

"44A Information where restriction direction not given

"44A Information where restriction direction not given

(1) This section applies if, in a case where section 42 applies, the transfer direction in respect of the patient was given without a restriction direction.

(2) The responsible clinician must inform the managers of the relevant hospital—

(a) whether he is to make an order for discharge in respect of the patient under section 23(2) of the Mental Health Act 1983;

(b) whether he is to make a community treatment order in respect of the patient;

(c) if a community treatment order is to be made in respect of the patient, what conditions are to be specified in the order;

(d) if a community treatment order is in force in respect of the patient, of any variation to be made under section 17B(4) of the Mental Health Act 1983 of the conditions specified in the order;

(e) if a community treatment order in respect of the patient is to cease to be in force, of the date on which it is to cease to be in force;

(f) if, following the examination of the patient under section 20 of the Mental Health Act 1983, it does not appear to the responsible clinician that the conditions set out in subsection (4) of that section are satisfied, of the date on which the authority for the patient's detention is to expire.

(3) Any person who has power to make an order for discharge in respect of the patient under section 23(3) of the Mental Health Act 1983 must inform the managers of the relevant hospital if he is to make that order.

(4) Subsection (5) applies if—

(a) an application is made to a Mental Health Review Tribunal under section 66 or 69 of the Mental Health Act 1983,

(b) the patient's case is referred to a Mental Health Review Tribunal under section 67 of that Act, or

(c) the managers of the relevant hospital refer the patient's case to a Mental Health Review Tribunal under section 68 of that Act.

(5) The tribunal must inform the managers of the relevant hospital if it directs that the patient be discharged.

(6) Subsection (7) applies if a person who appears to the managers of the relevant hospital to be the victim of the offence or to act for the victim of the offence—

(a) when his wishes were ascertained under section 42(2), expressed a wish to receive the information specified in section 42(4), or

(b) has subsequently informed the managers of the relevant hospital that he wishes to receive that information.

(7) The managers of the relevant hospital order must take all reasonable steps—

(a) to inform that person whether the patient is to be discharged under section 23 or 72 of the Mental Health Act 1983;

(b) to inform that person whether a community treatment order is to be made in respect of the patient;

(c) if a community treatment order is to be made in respect of the patient and is to specify conditions which relate to contact with the victim or his family, to provide that person with details of those conditions;

(d) if a community treatment order is in force in respect of the patient and the conditions specified in the order are to be varied under section 17B(4) of the Mental Health Act 1983, to provide that person with details of any variation which relates to contact with the victim or his family;

(e) if a community treatment order in respect of the patient is to cease to be in force, to inform that person of the date on which it is to cease to be in force;

(f) if, following the examination of the patient under section 20 of the Mental Health Act 1983, the authority for the patient's detention is not to be renewed, to inform that person of the date on which the authority is to expire;

(g) to provide that person with such other information as the managers of the relevant hospital consider appropriate in all the circumstances of the case.

(8) The relevant hospital has the meaning given by section 36A(6).

44B Removal of restriction

44B Removal of restriction

(1) This section applies if, in a case where section 42 applies—

(a) the transfer direction in respect of the patient was given with a restriction direction, and

(b) the restriction direction ceases to be in force while the transfer direction continues in force.

(2) Subsection (3) applies if a person who appears to the relevant local probation board to be the victim of the offence or to act for the victim of the offence—

(a) when his wishes were ascertained under section 42(2), expressed a wish to make representations about a matter specified in section 42(3) or to receive the information specified in section 42(4), or

(b) has subsequently informed the relevant local probation board that he wishes to make representations about such a matter or to receive that information.

(3) The relevant local probation board must take all reasonable steps—

(a) to notify the managers of the relevant hospital of an address at which that person may be contacted;

(b) to notify that person of the name and address of the hospital.

(4) While the transfer direction continues in force, the patient is to be regarded as a patient in respect of whom a transfer direction was given without a restriction direction; and sections 43A and 44A are to apply in relation to him accordingly.

(5) The relevant hospital has the meaning given in section 36A(6).

(6) The relevant local probation board has the meaning given in section 43(8)."

Interpretation

16 (1) Section 45 (the title to which becomes "Interpretation: sections 35 to 44B") is amended as follows.

(2) In subsection (1)—

(a) for "44" substitute "44B", and

(b) at the appropriate places insert—

"""community treatment order" has the meaning given in section 17A of the Mental Health Act 1983;",

"""the managers" has the meaning given in section 145 of the Mental Health Act 1983;",

"""responsible clinician" means the responsible clinician for the purposes of Part 3 of the Mental Health Act 1983;", and

"""responsible hospital" has the meaning given in section 17A of the Mental Health Act 1983;".

(3) In subsection (2), for "44" substitute "44B".

(4) After subsection (2) insert—

"(3) A reference in sections 35 to 44B to a place in which a person is detained includes a reference to a place in which he is liable to be detained under the Mental Health Act 1983.

(4) For the purposes of section 32(3) of that Act (regulations as to delegation of managers' functions, etc.) as applied by Parts 1 and 2 of Schedule 1 to that Act, a function conferred on the managers of a hospital under sections 35 to 44B of this Act is to be treated as a function of theirs under Part 3 of that Act."

SCHEDULE 7

Section 50

MENTAL CAPACITY ACT 2005: NEW SCHEDULE A1

Before Schedule 1 to the Mental Capacity Act 2005 (c. 9) insert—

"SCHEDULE A1

HOSPITAL AND CARE HOME RESIDENTS: DEPRIVATION OF LIBERTY

PART 1

AUTHORISATION TO DEPRIVE RESIDENTS OF LIBERTY ETC

1 Application of Part

1 (1) This Part applies if the following conditions are met.

(2) The first condition is that a person ("P") is detained in a hospital or care home — for the purpose of being given care or treatment — in circumstances which amount to deprivation of the person's liberty.

(3) The second condition is that a standard or urgent authorisation is in force.

(4) The third condition is that the standard or urgent authorisation relates—

(a) to P, and
(b) to the hospital or care home in which P is detained.

2 Authorisation to deprive P of liberty

2 The managing authority of the hospital or care home may deprive P of his liberty by detaining him as mentioned in paragraph 1(2).

3 No liability for acts done for purpose of depriving P of liberty

3 (1) This paragraph applies to any act which a person ("D") does for the purpose of detaining P as mentioned in paragraph 1(2).

(2) D does not incur any liability in relation to the act that he would not have incurred if P—

(a) had had capacity to consent in relation to D's doing the act, and
(b) had consented to D's doing the act.

4 No protection for negligent acts etc

4 (1) Paragraphs 2 and 3 do not exclude a person's civil liability for loss or damage, or his criminal liability, resulting from his negligence in doing any thing.

(2) Paragraphs 2 and 3 do not authorise a person to do anything otherwise than for the purpose of the standard or urgent authorisation that is in force.

(3) In a case where a standard authorisation is in force, paragraphs 2 and 3 do not authorise a person to do anything which does not comply with the conditions (if any) included in the authorisation.

PART 2

INTERPRETATION: MAIN TERMS

5 Introduction

5 This Part applies for the purposes of this Schedule.

6 Detained resident

6 "Detained resident" means a person detained in a hospital or care home — for the purpose of being given care or treatment — in circumstances which amount to deprivation of the person's liberty.

7 Relevant person etc

7 In relation to a person who is, or is to be, a detained resident—

"relevant person" means the person in question;

"relevant hospital or care home" means the hospital or care home in question;

"relevant care or treatment" means the care or treatment in question.

8 Authorisations

8 "Standard authorisation" means an authorisation given under Part 4.

9 "Urgent authorisation" means an authorisation given under Part 5.

10 "Authorisation under this Schedule" means either of the following—

(a) a standard authorisation;

(b) an urgent authorisation.

11 (1) The purpose of a standard authorisation is the purpose which is stated in the authorisation in accordance with paragraph 55(1)(d).

(2) The purpose of an urgent authorisation is the purpose which is stated in the authorisation in accordance with paragraph 80(d).

PART 3

THE QUALIFYING REQUIREMENTS

12 The qualifying requirements

12 (1) These are the qualifying requirements referred to in this Schedule—

(a) the age requirement;

(b) the mental health requirement;

(c) the mental capacity requirement;

(d) the best interests requirement;

(e) the eligibility requirement;

(f) the no refusals requirement.

(2) Any question of whether a person who is, or is to be, a detained resident meets the qualifying requirements is to be determined in accordance with this Part.

(3) In a case where—

(a) the question of whether a person meets a particular qualifying requirement arises in relation to the giving of a standard authorisation, and

(b) any circumstances relevant to determining that question are expected to change between the time when the determination is made and the time when the authorisation is expected to come into force,

those circumstances are to be taken into account as they are expected to be at the later time.

13 The age requirement

13 The relevant person meets the age requirement if he has reached 18.

14 The mental health requirement

14 (1) The relevant person meets the mental health requirement if he is suffering from mental disorder (within the meaning of the Mental Health Act, but disregarding any exclusion for persons with learning disability).

(2) An exclusion for persons with learning disability is any provision of the Mental Health Act which provides for a person with learning disability not to be regarded as suffering from mental disorder for one or more purposes of that Act.

15 The mental capacity requirement

15 The relevant person meets the mental capacity requirement if he lacks capacity in relation to the question whether or not he should be accommodated in the relevant hospital or care home for the purpose of being given the relevant care or treatment.

16 The best interests requirement

16 (1) The relevant person meets the best interests requirement if all of the following conditions are met.

(2) The first condition is that the relevant person is, or is to be, a detained resident.

(3) The second condition is that it is in the best interests of the relevant person for him to be a detained resident.

(4) The third condition is that, in order to prevent harm to the relevant person, it is necessary for him to be a detained resident.

(5) The fourth condition is that it is a proportionate response to—

(a) the likelihood of the relevant person suffering harm, and

(b) the seriousness of that harm,

for him to be a detained resident.

17 The eligibility requirement

17 (1) The relevant person meets the eligibility requirement unless he is ineligible to be deprived of liberty by this Act.

(2) Schedule 1A applies for the purpose of determining whether or not P is ineligible to be deprived of liberty by this Act.

18 The no refusals requirement

18 The relevant person meets the no refusals requirement unless there is a refusal within the meaning of paragraph 19 or 20.

19 (1) There is a refusal if these conditions are met—

(a) the relevant person has made an advance decision;

(b) the advance decision is valid;

(c) the advance decision is applicable to some or all of the relevant treatment.

(2) Expressions used in this paragraph and any of sections 24, 25 or 26 have the same meaning in this paragraph as in that section.

20 (1) There is a refusal if it would be in conflict with a valid decision of a donee or deputy for the relevant person to be accommodated in the relevant hospital or care home for the purpose of receiving some or all of the relevant care or treatment—

(a) in circumstances which amount to deprivation of the person's liberty, or

(b) at all.

(2) A donee is a donee of a lasting power of attorney granted by the relevant person.

(3) A decision of a donee or deputy is valid if it is made—

(a) within the scope of his authority as donee or deputy, and

(b) in accordance with Part 1 of this Act.

PART 4

STANDARD AUTHORISATIONS

21 Supervisory body to give authorisation

21 Only the supervisory body may give a standard authorisation.

22 The supervisory body may not give a standard authorisation unless—

(a) the managing authority of the relevant hospital or care home have requested it, or

(b) paragraph 71 applies (right of third party to require consideration of whether authorisation needed).

23 The managing authority may not make a request for a standard authorisation unless—

(a) they are required to do so by paragraph 24 (as read with paragraphs 27 to 29),

(b) they are required to do so by paragraph 25 (as read with paragraph 28), or

(c) they are permitted to do so by paragraph 30.

24 Duty to request authorisation: basic cases

24 (1) The managing authority must request a standard authorisation in any of the following cases.

(2) The first case is where it appears to the managing authority that the relevant person—

(a) is not yet accommodated in the relevant hospital or care home,

(b) is likely — at some time within the next 28 days — to be a detained resident in the relevant hospital or care home, and

(c) is likely—

(i) at that time, or

(ii) at some later time within the next 28 days,

to meet all of the qualifying requirements.

(3) The second case is where it appears to the managing authority that the relevant person—

(a) is already accommodated in the relevant hospital or care home,

(b) is likely — at some time within the next 28 days — to be a detained resident in the relevant hospital or care home, and

(c) is likely—

(i) at that time, or

(ii) at some later time within the next 28 days,

to meet all of the qualifying requirements.

(4) The third case is where it appears to the managing authority that the relevant person—

(a) is a detained resident in the relevant hospital or care home, and

(b) meets all of the qualifying requirements, or is likely to do so at some time within the next 28 days.

(5) This paragraph is subject to paragraphs 27 to 29.

25 Duty to request authorisation: change in place of detention

25 (1) The relevant managing authority must request a standard authorisation if it appears to them that these conditions are met.

(2) The first condition is that a standard authorisation—

(a) has been given, and

(b) has not ceased to be in force.

(3) The second condition is that there is, or is to be, a change in the place of detention.

(4) This paragraph is subject to paragraph 28.

26 (1) This paragraph applies for the purposes of paragraph 25.

(2) There is a change in the place of detention if the relevant person—

(a) ceases to be a detained resident in the stated hospital or care home, and

(b) becomes a detained resident in a different hospital or care home ("the new hospital or care home").

(3) The stated hospital or care home is the hospital or care home to which the standard authorisation relates.

(4) The relevant managing authority are the managing authority of the new hospital or care home.

27 Other authority for detention: request for authorisation

27 (1) This paragraph applies if, by virtue of section 4A(3), a decision of the court authorises the relevant person to be a detained resident.

(2) Paragraph 24 does not require a request for a standard authorisation to be made in relation to that detention unless these conditions are met.

(3) The first condition is that the standard authorisation would be in force at a time immediately after the expiry of the other authority.

(4) The second condition is that the standard authorisation would not be in force at any time on or before the expiry of the other authority.

(5) The third condition is that it would, in the managing authority's view, be unreasonable to delay making the request until a time nearer the expiry of the other authority.

(6) In this paragraph—

(a) the other authority is—

(i) the decision mentioned in sub-paragraph (1), or

(ii) any further decision of the court which, by virtue of section 4A(3), authorises, or is expected to authorise, the relevant person to be a detained resident;

(b) the expiry of the other authority is the time when the other authority is expected to cease to authorise the relevant person to be a detained resident.

28 Request refused: no further request unless change of circumstances

28 (1) This paragraph applies if—

(a) a managing authority request a standard authorisation under paragraph 24 or 25, and

(b) the supervisory body are prohibited by paragraph 50(2) from giving the authorisation.

(2) Paragraph 24 or 25 does not require that managing authority to make a new request for a standard authorisation unless it appears to the managing authority that—

(a) there has been a change in the relevant person's case, and

(b) because of that change, the supervisory body are likely to give a standard authorisation if requested.

29 Authorisation given: request for further authorisation

29 (1) This paragraph applies if a standard authorisation—

(a) has been given in relation to the detention of the relevant person, and

(b) that authorisation ("the existing authorisation") has not ceased to be in force.

(2) Paragraph 24 does not require a new request for a standard authorisation ("the new authorisation") to be made unless these conditions are met.

(3) The first condition is that the new authorisation would be in force at a time immediately after the expiry of the existing authorisation.

(4) The second condition is that the new authorisation would not be in force at any time on or before the expiry of the existing authorisation.

(5) The third condition is that it would, in the managing authority's view, be unreasonable to delay making the request until a time nearer the expiry of the existing authorisation.

(6) The expiry of the existing authorisation is the time when it is expected to cease to be in force.

30 Power to request authorisation

30 (1) This paragraph applies if—

(a) a standard authorisation has been given in relation to the detention of the relevant person,

(b) that authorisation ("the existing authorisation") has not ceased to be in force,

(c) the requirement under paragraph 24 to make a request for a new standard authorisation does not apply, because of paragraph 29, and

(d) a review of the existing authorisation has been requested, or is being carried out, in accordance with Part 8.

(2) The managing authority may request a new standard authorisation which would be in force on or before the expiry of the existing authorisation; but only if it would also be in force immediately after that expiry.

(3) The expiry of the existing authorisation is the time when it is expected to cease to be in force.

(4) Further provision relating to cases where a request is made under this paragraph can be found in—

(a) paragraph 62 (effect of decision about request), and

(b) paragraph 124 (effect of request on Part 8 review).

31 Information included in request

31 A request for a standard authorisation must include the information (if any) required by regulations.

32 Records of requests

32 (1) The managing authority of a hospital or care home must keep a written record of—

(a) each request that they make for a standard authorisation, and

(b) the reasons for making each request.

(2) A supervisory body must keep a written record of each request for a standard authorisation that is made to them.

33 Relevant person must be assessed

33 (1) This paragraph applies if the supervisory body are requested to give a standard authorisation.

(2) The supervisory body must secure that all of these assessments are carried out in relation to the relevant person—

(a) an age assessment;

(b) a mental health assessment;

(c) a mental capacity assessment;

(d) a best interests assessment;

(e) an eligibility assessment;

(f) a no refusals assessment.

(3) The person who carries out any such assessment is referred to as the assessor.

(4) Regulations may be made about the period (or periods) within which assessors must carry out assessments.

(5) This paragraph is subject to paragraphs 49 and 133.

34 Age assessment

34 An age assessment is an assessment of whether the relevant person meets the age requirement.

35 Mental health assessment

35 A mental health assessment is an assessment of whether the relevant person meets the mental health requirement.

36 When carrying out a mental health assessment, the assessor must also—

(a) consider how (if at all) the relevant person's mental health is likely to be affected by his being a detained resident, and

(b) notify the best interests assessor of his conclusions.

37 Mental capacity assessment

37 A mental capacity assessment is an assessment of whether the relevant person meets the mental capacity requirement.

38 Best interests assessment

38 A best interests assessment is an assessment of whether the relevant person meets the best interests requirement.

39 (1) In carrying out a best interests assessment, the assessor must comply with the duties in sub-paragraphs (2) and (3).

(2) The assessor must consult the managing authority of the relevant hospital or care home.

(3) The assessor must have regard to all of the following—

(a) the conclusions which the mental health assessor has notified to the best interests assessor in accordance with paragraph 36(b);

(b) any relevant needs assessment;

(c) any relevant care plan.

(4) A relevant needs assessment is an assessment of the relevant person's needs which—

(a) was carried out in connection with the relevant person being accommodated in the relevant hospital or care home, and

(b) was carried out by or on behalf of—

(i) the managing authority of the relevant hospital or care home, or

(ii) the supervisory body.

(5) A relevant care plan is a care plan which—

(a) sets out how the relevant person's needs are to be met whilst he is accommodated in the relevant hospital or care home, and

(b) was drawn up by or on behalf of—

(i) the managing authority of the relevant hospital or care home, or

(ii) the supervisory body.

(6) The managing authority must give the assessor a copy of—

(a) any relevant needs assessment carried out by them or on their behalf, or

(b) any relevant care plan drawn up by them or on their behalf.

(7) The supervisory body must give the assessor a copy of—

(a) any relevant needs assessment carried out by them or on their behalf, or

(b) any relevant care plan drawn up by them or on their behalf.

(8) The duties in sub-paragraphs (2) and (3) do not affect any other duty to consult or to take the views of others into account.

40 (1) This paragraph applies whatever conclusion the best interests assessment comes to.

(2) The assessor must state in the best interests assessment the name and address of every interested person whom he has consulted in carrying out the assessment.

41 Paragraphs 42 and 43 apply if the best interests assessment comes to the conclusion that the relevant person meets the best interests requirement.

42 (1) The assessor must state in the assessment the maximum authorisation period.

(2) The maximum authorisation period is the shorter of these periods—

(a) the period which, in the assessor's opinion, would be the appropriate maximum period for the relevant person to be a detained resident under the standard authorisation that has been requested;

(b) 1 year, or such shorter period as may be prescribed in regulations.

(3) Regulations under sub-paragraph (2)(b)—

(a) need not provide for a shorter period to apply in relation to all standard authorisations;

(b) may provide for different periods to apply in relation to different kinds of standard authorisations.

(4) Before making regulations under sub-paragraph (2)(b) the Secretary of State must consult all of the following—

(a) each body required by regulations under paragraph 162 to monitor and report on the operation of this Schedule in relation to England;

(b) such other persons as the Secretary of State considers it appropriate to consult.

(5) Before making regulations under sub-paragraph (2)(b) the National Assembly for Wales must consult all of the following—

(a) each person or body directed under paragraph 163(2) to carry out any function of the Assembly of monitoring and reporting on the operation of this Schedule in relation to Wales;

(b) such other persons as the Assembly considers it appropriate to consult.

43 The assessor may include in the assessment recommendations about conditions to which the standard authorisation is, or is not, to be subject in accordance with paragraph 53.

44 (1) This paragraph applies if the best interests assessment comes to the conclusion that the relevant person does not meet the best interests requirement.

(2) If, on the basis of the information taken into account in carrying out the assessment, it appears to the assessor that there is an unauthorised deprivation of liberty, he must include a statement to that effect in the assessment.

(3) There is an unauthorised deprivation of liberty if the managing authority of the relevant hospital or care home are already depriving the relevant person of his liberty without authority of the kind mentioned in section 4A.

45 The duties with which the best interests assessor must comply are subject to the provision included in appointment regulations under Part 10 (in particular, provision made under paragraph 146).

46 Eligibility assessment

46 An eligibility assessment is an assessment of whether the relevant person meets the eligibility requirement.

47 (1) Regulations may—

(a) require an eligibility assessor to request a best interests assessor to provide relevant eligibility information, and

(b) require the best interests assessor, if such a request is made, to provide such relevant eligibility information as he may have.

(2) In this paragraph—

"best interests assessor" means any person who is carrying out, or has carried out, a best interests assessment in relation to the relevant person;

"eligibility assessor" means a person carrying out an eligibility assessment in relation to the relevant person;

"relevant eligibility information" is information relevant to assessing whether or not the relevant person is ineligible by virtue of paragraph 5 of Schedule 1A.

48 No refusals assessment

48 A no refusals assessment is an assessment of whether the relevant person meets the no refusals requirement.

49 Equivalent assessment already carried out

49 (1) The supervisory body are not required by paragraph 33 to secure that a particular kind of assessment ("the required assessment") is carried out in relation to the relevant person if the following conditions are met.

(2) The first condition is that the supervisory body have a written copy of an assessment of the relevant person ("the existing assessment") that has already been carried out.

(3) The second condition is that the existing assessment complies with all requirements under this Schedule with which the required assessment would have to comply (if it were carried out).

(4) The third condition is that the existing assessment was carried out within the previous 12 months; but this condition need not be met if the required assessment is an age assessment.

(5) The fourth condition is that the supervisory body are satisfied that there is no reason why the existing assessment may no longer be accurate.

(6) If the required assessment is a best interests assessment, in satisfying themselves as mentioned in sub-paragraph (5), the supervisory body must take into account any information given, or submissions made, by—

(a) the relevant person's representative,

(b) any section 39C IMCA, or

(c) any section 39D IMCA.

(7) It does not matter whether the existing assessment was carried out in connection with a request for a standard authorisation or for some other purpose.

(8) If, because of this paragraph, the supervisory body are not required by paragraph 33 to secure that the required assessment is carried out, the existing assessment is to be treated for the purposes of this Schedule—

(a) as an assessment of the same kind as the required assessment, and

(b) as having been carried out under paragraph 33 in connection with the request for the standard authorisation.

50 Duty to give authorisation

50 (1) The supervisory body must give a standard authorisation if—

(a) all assessments are positive, and

(b) the supervisory body have written copies of all those assessments.

(2) The supervisory body must not give a standard authorisation except in accordance with sub-paragraph (1).

(3) All assessments are positive if each assessment carried out under paragraph 33 has come to the conclusion that the relevant person meets the qualifying requirement to which the assessment relates.

51 Terms of authorisation

51 (1) If the supervisory body are required to give a standard authorisation, they must decide the period during which the authorisation is to be in force.

(2) That period must not exceed the maximum authorisation period stated in the best interests assessment.

52 A standard authorisation may provide for the authorisation to come into force at a time after it is given.

53 (1) A standard authorisation may be given subject to conditions.

(2) Before deciding whether to give the authorisation subject to conditions, the supervisory body must have regard to any recommendations in the best interests assessment about such conditions.

(3) The managing authority of the relevant hospital or care home must ensure that any conditions are complied with.

54 Form of authorisation

54 A standard authorisation must be in writing.

55 (1) A standard authorisation must state the following things—

(a) the name of the relevant person;

(b) the name of the relevant hospital or care home;

(c) the period during which the authorisation is to be in force;

(d) the purpose for which the authorisation is given;

(e) any conditions subject to which the authorisation is given;

(f) the reason why each qualifying requirement is met.

(2) The statement of the reason why the eligibility requirement is met must be framed by reference to the cases in the table in paragraph 2 of Schedule 1A.

56 (1) If the name of the relevant hospital or care home changes, the standard authorisation is to be read as if it stated the current name of the hospital or care home.

(2) But sub-paragraph (1) is subject to any provision relating to the change of name which is made in any enactment or in any instrument made under an enactment.

57 Duty to give information about decision

57 (1) This paragraph applies if—

(a) a request is made for a standard authorisation, and

(b) the supervisory body are required by paragraph 50(1) to give the standard authorisation.

(2) The supervisory body must give a copy of the authorisation to each of the following—

(a) the relevant person's representative;

(b) the managing authority of the relevant hospital or care home;

(c) the relevant person;

(d) any section 39A IMCA;

(e) every interested person consulted by the best interests assessor.

(3) The supervisory body must comply with this paragraph as soon as practicable after they give the standard authorisation.

58 (1) This paragraph applies if—

(a) a request is made for a standard authorisation, and

(b) the supervisory body are prohibited by paragraph 50(2) from giving the standard authorisation.

(2) The supervisory body must give notice, stating that they are prohibited from giving the authorisation, to each of the following—

(a) the managing authority of the relevant hospital or care home;

(b) the relevant person;

(c) any section 39A IMCA;

(d) every interested person consulted by the best interests assessor.

(3) The supervisory body must comply with this paragraph as soon as practicable after it becomes apparent to them that they are prohibited from giving the authorisation.

59 Duty to give information about effect of authorisation

59 (1) This paragraph applies if a standard authorisation is given.

(2) The managing authority of the relevant hospital or care home must take such steps as are practicable to ensure that the relevant person understands all of the following—

(a) the effect of the authorisation;

(b) the right to make an application to the court to exercise its jurisdiction under section 21A;
(c) the right under Part 8 to request a review;
(d) the right to have a section 39D IMCA appointed;
(e) how to have a section 39D IMCA appointed.

(3) Those steps must be taken as soon as is practicable after the authorisation is given.

(4) Those steps must include the giving of appropriate information both orally and in writing.

(5) Any written information given to the relevant person must also be given by the managing authority to the relevant person's representative.

(6) They must give the information to the representative as soon as is practicable after it is given to the relevant person.

(7) Sub-paragraph (8) applies if the managing authority is notified that a section 39D IMCA has been appointed.

(8) As soon as is practicable after being notified, the managing authority must give the section 39D IMCA a copy of the written information given in accordance with sub-paragraph (4).

60 Records of authorisations

60 A supervisory body must keep a written record of all of the following information—
(a) the standard authorisations that they have given;
(b) the requests for standard authorisations in response to which they have not given an authorisation;
(c) in relation to each standard authorisation given: the matters stated in the authorisation in accordance with paragraph 55.

61 Variation of an authorisation

61 (1) A standard authorisation may not be varied except in accordance with Part 7 or 8.

(2) This paragraph does not affect the powers of the Court of Protection or of any other court.

62 Effect of decision about request made under paragraph 25 or 30

62 (1) This paragraph applies where the managing authority request a new standard authorisation under either of the following—
(a) paragraph 25 (change in place of detention);
(b) paragraph 30 (existing authorisation subject to review).

(2) If the supervisory body are required by paragraph 50(1) to give the new authorisation, the existing authorisation terminates at the time when the new authorisation comes into force.

(3) If the supervisory body are prohibited by paragraph 50(2) from giving the new authorisation, there is no effect on the existing authorisation's continuation in force.

63 When an authorisation is in force

63 (1) A standard authorisation comes into force when it is given.

(2) But if the authorisation provides for it to come into force at a later time, it comes into force at that time.

64 (1) A standard authorisation ceases to be in force at the end of the period stated in the authorisation in accordance with paragraph 55(1)(c).

(2) But if the authorisation terminates before then in accordance with paragraph 62(2) or any other provision of this Schedule, it ceases to be in force when the termination takes effect.

(3) This paragraph does not affect the powers of the Court of Protection or of any other court.

65 (1) This paragraph applies if a standard authorisation ceases to be in force.

(2) The supervisory body must give notice that the authorisation has ceased to be in force.

(3) The supervisory body must give that notice to all of the following—

- (a) the managing authority of the relevant hospital or care home;
- (b) the relevant person;
- (c) the relevant person's representative;
- (d) every interested person consulted by the best interests assessor.

(4) The supervisory body must give that notice as soon as practicable after the authorisation ceases to be in force.

66 When a request for a standard authorisation is "disposed of"

66 A request for a standard authorisation is to be regarded for the purposes of this Schedule as disposed of if the supervisory body have given—

- (a) a copy of the authorisation in accordance with paragraph 57, or
- (b) notice in accordance with paragraph 58.

67 Right of third party to require consideration of whether authorisation needed

67 For the purposes of paragraphs 68 to 73 there is an unauthorised deprivation of liberty if—

- (a) a person is already a detained resident in a hospital or care home, and
- (b) the detention of the person is not authorised as mentioned in section 4A.

68 (1) If the following conditions are met, an eligible person may request the supervisory body to decide whether or not there is an unauthorised deprivation of liberty.

(2) The first condition is that the eligible person has notified the managing authority of the relevant hospital or care home that it appears to the eligible person that there is an unauthorised deprivation of liberty.

(3) The second condition is that the eligible person has asked the managing authority to request a standard authorisation in relation to the detention of the relevant person.

(4) The third condition is that the managing authority has not requested a standard authorisation within a reasonable period after the eligible person asks it to do so.

(5) In this paragraph "eligible person" means any person other than the managing authority of the relevant hospital or care home.

69 (1) This paragraph applies if an eligible person requests the supervisory body to decide whether or not there is an unauthorised deprivation of liberty.

(2) The supervisory body must select and appoint a person to carry out an assessment of whether or not the relevant person is a detained resident.

(3) But the supervisory body need not select and appoint a person to carry out such an assessment in either of these cases.

(4) The first case is where it appears to the supervisory body that the request by the eligible person is frivolous or vexatious.

(5) The second case is where it appears to the supervisory body that—

- (a) the question of whether or not there is an unauthorised deprivation of liberty has already been decided, and
- (b) since that decision, there has been no change of circumstances which would merit the question being decided again.

(6) The supervisory body must not select and appoint a person to carry out an assessment under this paragraph unless it appears to the supervisory body that the person would be—

- (a) suitable to carry out a best interests assessment (if one were obtained in connection with a request for a standard authorisation relating to the relevant person), and
- (b) eligible to carry out such a best interests assessment.

(7) The supervisory body must notify the persons specified in sub-paragraph (8)—

- (a) that the supervisory body have been requested to decide whether or not there is an unauthorised deprivation of liberty;
- (b) of their decision whether or not to select and appoint a person to carry out an assessment under this paragraph;
- (c) if their decision is to select and appoint a person, of the person appointed.

(8) The persons referred to in sub-paragraph (7) are—

- (a) the eligible person who made the request under paragraph 68;
- (b) the person to whom the request relates;
- (c) the managing authority of the relevant hospital or care home;
- (d) any section 39A IMCA.

70 (1) Regulations may be made about the period within which an assessment under paragraph 69 must be carried out.

(2) Regulations made under paragraph 129(3) apply in relation to the selection and appointment of a person under paragraph 69 as they apply to the selection of a person under paragraph 129 to carry out a best interests assessment.

(3) The following provisions apply to an assessment under paragraph 69 as they apply to an assessment carried out in connection with a request for a standard authorisation—

(a) paragraph 131 (examination and copying of records);
(b) paragraph 132 (representations);
(c) paragraphs 134 and 135(1) and (2) (duty to keep records and give copies).

(4) The copies of the assessment which the supervisory body are required to give under paragraph 135(2) must be given as soon as practicable after the supervisory body are themselves given a copy of the assessment.

71 (1) This paragraph applies if—
(a) the supervisory body obtain an assessment under paragraph 69,
(b) the assessment comes to the conclusion that the relevant person is a detained resident, and
(c) it appears to the supervisory body that the detention of the person is not authorised as mentioned in section 4A.

(2) This Schedule (including Part 5) applies as if the managing authority of the relevant hospital or care home had, in accordance with Part 4, requested the supervisory body to give a standard authorisation in relation to the relevant person.

(3) The managing authority of the relevant hospital or care home must supply the supervisory body with the information (if any) which the managing authority would, by virtue of paragraph 31, have had to include in a request for a standard authorisation.

(4) The supervisory body must notify the persons specified in paragraph 69(8)—
(a) of the outcome of the assessment obtained under paragraph 69, and
(b) that this Schedule applies as mentioned in sub-paragraph (2).

72 (1) This paragraph applies if—
(a) the supervisory body obtain an assessment under paragraph 69, and
(b) the assessment comes to the conclusion that the relevant person is not a detained resident.

(2) The supervisory body must notify the persons specified in paragraph 69(8) of the outcome of the assessment.

73 (1) This paragraph applies if—
(a) the supervisory body obtain an assessment under paragraph 69,
(b) the assessment comes to the conclusion that the relevant person is a detained resident, and
(c) it appears to the supervisory body that the detention of the person is authorised as mentioned in section 4A.

(2) The supervisory body must notify the persons specified in paragraph 69(8)—
(a) of the outcome of the assessment, and
(b) that it appears to the supervisory body that the detention is authorised.

PART 5

URGENT AUTHORISATIONS

74 Managing authority to give authorisation

74 Only the managing authority of the relevant hospital or care home may give an urgent authorisation.

75 The managing authority may give an urgent authorisation only if they are required to do so by paragraph 76 (as read with paragraph 77).

76 Duty to give authorisation

76 (1) The managing authority must give an urgent authorisation in either of the following cases.

(2) The first case is where—

(a) the managing authority are required to make a request under paragraph 24 or 25 for a standard authorisation, and

(b) they believe that the need for the relevant person to be a detained resident is so urgent that it is appropriate for the detention to begin before they make the request.

(3) The second case is where—

(a) the managing authority have made a request under paragraph 24 or 25 for a standard authorisation, and

(b) they believe that the need for the relevant person to be a detained resident is so urgent that it is appropriate for the detention to begin before the request is disposed of.

(4) References in this paragraph to the detention of the relevant person are references to the detention to which paragraph 24 or 25 relates.

(5) This paragraph is subject to paragraph 77.

77 (1) This paragraph applies where the managing authority have given an urgent authorisation ("the original authorisation") in connection with a case where a person is, or is to be, a detained resident ("the existing detention").

(2) No new urgent authorisation is to be given under paragraph 76 in connection with the existing detention.

(3) But the managing authority may request the supervisory body to extend the duration of the original authorisation.

(4) Only one request under sub-paragraph (3) may be made in relation to the original authorisation.

(5) Paragraphs 84 to 86 apply to any request made under sub-paragraph (3).

78 Terms of authorisation

78 (1) If the managing authority decide to give an urgent authorisation, they must decide the period during which the authorisation is to be in force.

(2) That period must not exceed 7 days.

79 Form of authorisation

79 An urgent authorisation must be in writing.

80 An urgent authorisation must state the following things—

(a) the name of the relevant person;

(b) the name of the relevant hospital or care home;

(c) the period during which the authorisation is to be in force;

(d) the purpose for which the authorisation is given.

81 (1) If the name of the relevant hospital or care home changes, the urgent authorisation is to be read as if it stated the current name of the hospital or care home.

(2) But sub-paragraph (1) is subject to any provision relating to the change of name which is made in any enactment or in any instrument made under an enactment.

82 Duty to keep records and give copies

82 (1) This paragraph applies if an urgent authorisation is given.

(2) The managing authority must keep a written record of why they have given the urgent authorisation.

(3) As soon as practicable after giving the authorisation, the managing authority must give a copy of the authorisation to all of the following—

(a) the relevant person;

(b) any section 39A IMCA.

83 Duty to give information about authorisation

83 (1) This paragraph applies if an urgent authorisation is given.

(2) The managing authority of the relevant hospital or care home must take such steps as are practicable to ensure that the relevant person understands all of the following—

(a) the effect of the authorisation;

(b) the right to make an application to the court to exercise its jurisdiction under section 21A.

(3) Those steps must be taken as soon as is practicable after the authorisation is given.

(4) Those steps must include the giving of appropriate information both orally and in writing.

84 Request for extension of duration

84 (1) This paragraph applies if the managing authority make a request under paragraph 77 for the supervisory body to extend the duration of the original authorisation.

(2) The managing authority must keep a written record of why they have made the request.

(3) The managing authority must give the relevant person notice that they have made the request.

(4) The supervisory body may extend the duration of the original authorisation if it appears to them that—

(a) the managing authority have made the required request for a standard authorisation,

(b) there are exceptional reasons why it has not yet been possible for that request to be disposed of, and

(c) it is essential for the existing detention to continue until the request is disposed of.

(5) The supervisory body must keep a written record that the request has been made to them.

(6) In this paragraph and paragraphs 85 and 86—

(a) "original authorisation" and "existing detention" have the same meaning as in paragraph 77;

(b) the required request for a standard authorisation is the request that is referred to in paragraph 76(2) or (3).

85 (1) This paragraph applies if, under paragraph 84, the supervisory body decide to extend the duration of the original authorisation.

(2) The supervisory body must decide the period of the extension.

(3) That period must not exceed 7 days.

(4) The supervisory body must give the managing authority notice stating the period of the extension.

(5) The managing authority must then vary the original authorisation so that it states the extended duration.

(6) Paragraphs 82(3) and 83 apply (with the necessary modifications) to the variation of the original authorisation as they apply to the giving of an urgent authorisation.

(7) The supervisory body must keep a written record of—

(a) the outcome of the request, and

(b) the period of the extension.

86 (1) This paragraph applies if, under paragraph 84, the supervisory body decide not to extend the duration of the original authorisation.

(2) The supervisory body must give the managing authority notice stating—

(a) the decision, and

(b) their reasons for making it.

(3) The managing authority must give a copy of that notice to all of the following—

(a) the relevant person;

(b) any section 39A IMCA.

(4) The supervisory body must keep a written record of the outcome of the request.

87 No variation

87 (1) An urgent authorisation may not be varied except in accordance with paragraph 85.

(2) This paragraph does not affect the powers of the Court of Protection or of any other court.

88 When an authorisation is in force

88 An urgent authorisation comes into force when it is given.

89 (1) An urgent authorisation ceases to be in force at the end of the period stated in the authorisation in accordance with paragraph 80(c) (subject to any variation in accordance with paragraph 85).

(2) But if the required request is disposed of before the end of that period, the urgent authorisation ceases to be in force as follows.

(3) If the supervisory body are required by paragraph 50(1) to give the requested authorisation, the urgent authorisation ceases to be in force when the requested authorisation comes into force.

(4) If the supervisory body are prohibited by paragraph 50(2) from giving the requested authorisation, the urgent authorisation ceases to be in force when the managing authority receive notice under paragraph 58.

(5) In this paragraph—

"required request" means the request referred to in paragraph 76(2) or (3);

"requested authorisation" means the standard authorisation to which the required request relates.

(6) This paragraph does not affect the powers of the Court of Protection or of any other court.

90 (1) This paragraph applies if an urgent authorisation ceases to be in force.

(2) The supervisory body must give notice that the authorisation has ceased to be in force.

(3) The supervisory body must give that notice to all of the following—

(a) the relevant person;

(b) any section 39A IMCA.

(4) The supervisory body must give that notice as soon as practicable after the authorisation ceases to be in force.

PART 6

ELIGIBILITY REQUIREMENT NOT MET: SUSPENSION OF STANDARD AUTHORISATION

91 (1) This Part applies if the following conditions are met.

(2) The first condition is that a standard authorisation—

(a) has been given, and

(b) has not ceased to be in force.

(3) The second condition is that the managing authority of the relevant hospital or care home are satisfied that the relevant person has ceased to meet the eligibility requirement.

(4) But this Part does not apply if the relevant person is ineligible by virtue of paragraph 5 of Schedule 1A (in which case see Part 8).

92 The managing authority of the relevant hospital or care home must give the supervisory body notice that the relevant person has ceased to meet the eligibility requirement.

93 (1) This paragraph applies if the managing authority give the supervisory body notice under paragraph 92.

(2) The standard authorisation is suspended from the time when the notice is given.

(3) The supervisory body must give notice that the standard authorisation has been suspended to the following persons—

(a) the relevant person;

(b) the relevant person's representative;

(c) the managing authority of the relevant hospital or care home.

94 (1) This paragraph applies if, whilst the standard authorisation is suspended, the managing authority are satisfied that the relevant person meets the eligibility requirement again.

(2) The managing authority must give the supervisory body notice that the relevant person meets the eligibility requirement again.

95 (1) This paragraph applies if the managing authority give the supervisory body notice under paragraph 94.

(2) The standard authorisation ceases to be suspended from the time when the notice is given.

(3) The supervisory body must give notice that the standard authorisation has ceased to be suspended to the following persons—

(a) the relevant person;

(b) the relevant person's representative;

(c) any section 39D IMCA;

(d) the managing authority of the relevant hospital or care home.

(4) The supervisory body must give notice under this paragraph as soon as practicable after they are given notice under paragraph 94.

96 (1) This paragraph applies if no notice is given under paragraph 94 before the end of the relevant 28 day period.

(2) The standard authorisation ceases to have effect at the end of the relevant 28 day period.

(3) The relevant 28 day period is the period of 28 days beginning with the day on which the standard authorisation is suspended under paragraph 93.

97 The effect of suspending the standard authorisation is that Part 1 ceases to apply for as long as the authorisation is suspended.

PART 7

STANDARD AUTHORISATIONS: CHANGE IN SUPERVISORY RESPONSIBILITY

98 Application of this Part

98 (1) This Part applies if these conditions are met.

(2) The first condition is that a standard authorisation—

(a) has been given, and

(b) has not ceased to be in force.

(3) The second condition is that there is a change in supervisory responsibility.

(4) The third condition is that there is not a change in the place of detention (within the meaning of paragraph 25).

99 For the purposes of this Part there is a change in supervisory responsibility if—

(a) one body ("the old supervisory body") have ceased to be supervisory body in relation to the standard authorisation, and

(b) a different body ("the new supervisory body") have become supervisory body in relation to the standard authorisation.

100 Effect of change in supervisory responsibility

100 (1) The new supervisory body becomes the supervisory body in relation to the authorisation.

(2) Anything done by or in relation to the old supervisory body in connection with the authorisation has effect, so far as is necessary for continuing its effect after the change, as if done by or in relation to the new supervisory body.

(3) Anything which relates to the authorisation and which is in the process of being done by or in relation to the old supervisory body at the time of the change may be continued by or in relation to the new supervisory body.

(4) But—

(a) the old supervisory body do not, by virtue of this paragraph, cease to be liable for anything done by them in connection with the authorisation before the change; and

(b) the new supervisory body do not, by virtue of this paragraph, become liable for any such thing.

PART 8

STANDARD AUTHORISATIONS: REVIEW

101 Application of this Part

101 (1) This Part applies if a standard authorisation—

(a) has been given, and

(b) has not ceased to be in force.

(2) Paragraphs 102 to 122 are subject to paragraphs 123 to 125.

102 Review by supervisory body

102 (1) The supervisory body may at any time carry out a review of the standard authorisation in accordance with this Part.

(2) The supervisory body must carry out such a review if they are requested to do so by an eligible person.

(3) Each of the following is an eligible person—

(a) the relevant person;

(b) the relevant person's representative;

(c) the managing authority of the relevant hospital or care home.

103 Request for review

103 (1) An eligible person may, at any time, request the supervisory body to carry out a review of the standard authorisation in accordance with this Part.

(2) The managing authority of the relevant hospital or care home must make such a request if one or more of the qualifying requirements appear to them to be reviewable.

104 Grounds for review

104 (1) Paragraphs 105 to 107 set out the grounds on which the qualifying requirements are reviewable.

(2) A qualifying requirement is not reviewable on any other ground.

105 Non-qualification ground

105 (1) Any of the following qualifying requirements is reviewable on the ground that the relevant person does not meet the requirement—

(a) the age requirement;

(b) the mental health requirement;

(c) the mental capacity requirement;

(d) the best interests requirement;

(e) the no refusals requirement.

(2) The eligibility requirement is reviewable on the ground that the relevant person is ineligible by virtue of paragraph 5 of Schedule 1A.

(3) The ground in sub-paragraph (1) and the ground in sub-paragraph (2) are referred to as the non-qualification ground.

106 Change of reason ground

106 (1) Any of the following qualifying requirements is reviewable on the ground set out in sub-paragraph (2)—

(a) the mental health requirement;

(b) the mental capacity requirement;
(c) the best interests requirement;
(d) the eligibility requirement;
(e) the no refusals requirement.

(2) The ground is that the reason why the relevant person meets the requirement is not the reason stated in the standard authorisation.

(3) This ground is referred to as the change of reason ground.

107 Variation of conditions ground

107 (1) The best interests requirement is reviewable on the ground that—
(a) there has been a change in the relevant person's case, and
(b) because of that change, it would be appropriate to vary the conditions to which the standard authorisation is subject.

(2) This ground is referred to as the variation of conditions ground.

(3) A reference to varying the conditions to which the standard authorisation is subject is a reference to—
(a) amendment of an existing condition,
(b) omission of an existing condition, or
(c) inclusion of a new condition (whether or not there are already any existing conditions).

108 Notice that review to be carried out

108 (1) If the supervisory body are to carry out a review of the standard authorisation, they must give notice of the review to the following persons—
(a) the relevant person;
(b) the relevant person's representative;
(c) the managing authority of the relevant hospital or care home.

(2) The supervisory body must give the notice—
(a) before they begin the review, or
(b) if that is not practicable, as soon as practicable after they have begun it.

(3) This paragraph does not require the supervisory body to give notice to any person who has requested the review.

109 Starting a review

109 To start a review of the standard authorisation, the supervisory body must decide which, if any, of the qualifying requirements appear to be reviewable.

110 No reviewable qualifying requirements

110 (1) This paragraph applies if no qualifying requirements appear to be reviewable.

(2) This Part does not require the supervisory body to take any action in respect of the standard authorisation.

111 One or more reviewable qualifying requirements

111 (1) This paragraph applies if one or more qualifying requirements appear to be reviewable.

(2) The supervisory body must secure that a separate review assessment is carried out in relation to each qualifying requirement which appears to be reviewable.

(3) But sub-paragraph (2) does not require the supervisory body to secure that a best interests review assessment is carried out in a case where the best interests requirement appears to the supervisory body to be non-assessable.

(4) The best interests requirement is non-assessable if—

(a) the requirement is reviewable only on the variation of conditions ground, and

(b) the change in the relevant person's case is not significant.

(5) In making any decision whether the change in the relevant person's case is significant, regard must be had to—

(a) the nature of the change, and

(b) the period that the change is likely to last for.

112 Review assessments

112 (1) A review assessment is an assessment of whether the relevant person meets a qualifying requirement.

(2) In relation to a review assessment—

(a) a negative conclusion is a conclusion that the relevant person does not meet the qualifying requirement to which the assessment relates;

(b) a positive conclusion is a conclusion that the relevant person meets the qualifying requirement to which the assessment relates.

(3) An age review assessment is a review assessment carried out in relation to the age requirement.

(4) A mental health review assessment is a review assessment carried out in relation to the mental health requirement.

(5) A mental capacity review assessment is a review assessment carried out in relation to the mental capacity requirement.

(6) A best interests review assessment is a review assessment carried out in relation to the best interests requirement.

(7) An eligibility review assessment is a review assessment carried out in relation to the eligibility requirement.

(8) A no refusals review assessment is a review assessment carried out in relation to the no refusals requirement.

113 (1) In carrying out a review assessment, the assessor must comply with any duties which would be imposed upon him under Part 4 if the assessment were being carried out in connection with a request for a standard authorisation.

(2) But in the case of a best interests review assessment, paragraphs 43 and 44 do not apply.

(3) Instead of what is required by paragraph 43, the best interests review assessment must include recommendations about whether — and, if so, how — it would be appropriate to vary the conditions to which the standard authorisation is subject.

114 Best interests requirement reviewable but non-assessable

114 (1) This paragraph applies in a case where—

(a) the best interests requirement appears to be reviewable, but

(b) in accordance with paragraph 111(3), the supervisory body are not required to secure that a best interests review assessment is carried out.

(2) The supervisory body may vary the conditions to which the standard authorisation is subject in such ways (if any) as the supervisory body think are appropriate in the circumstances.

115 Best interests review assessment positive

115 (1) This paragraph applies in a case where—

(a) a best interests review assessment is carried out, and

(b) the assessment comes to a positive conclusion.

(2) The supervisory body must decide the following questions—

(a) whether or not the best interests requirement is reviewable on the change of reason ground;

(b) whether or not the best interests requirement is reviewable on the variation of conditions ground;

(c) if so, whether or not the change in the person's case is significant.

(3) If the supervisory body decide that the best interests requirement is reviewable on the change of reason ground, they must vary the standard authorisation so that it states the reason why the relevant person now meets that requirement.

(4) If the supervisory body decide that—

(a) the best interests requirement is reviewable on the variation of conditions ground, and

(b) the change in the relevant person's case is not significant,

they may vary the conditions to which the standard authorisation is subject in such ways (if any) as they think are appropriate in the circumstances.

(5) If the supervisory body decide that—

(a) the best interests requirement is reviewable on the variation of conditions ground, and

(b) the change in the relevant person's case is significant,

they must vary the conditions to which the standard authorisation is subject in such ways as they think are appropriate in the circumstances.

(6) If the supervisory body decide that the best interests requirement is not reviewable on—

(a) the change of reason ground, or

(b) the variation of conditions ground,

this Part does not require the supervisory body to take any action in respect of the standard authorisation so far as the best interests requirement relates to it.

116 Mental health, mental capacity, eligibility or no refusals review assessment positive

116 (1) This paragraph applies if the following conditions are met.

(2) The first condition is that one or more of the following are carried out—
- (a) a mental health review assessment;
- (b) a mental capacity review assessment;
- (c) an eligibility review assessment;
- (d) a no refusals review assessment.

(3) The second condition is that each assessment carried out comes to a positive conclusion.

(4) The supervisory body must decide whether or not each of the assessed qualifying requirements is reviewable on the change of reason ground.

(5) If the supervisory body decide that any of the assessed qualifying requirements is reviewable on the change of reason ground, they must vary the standard authorisation so that it states the reason why the relevant person now meets the requirement or requirements in question.

(6) If the supervisory body decide that none of the assessed qualifying requirements are reviewable on the change of reason ground, this Part does not require the supervisory body to take any action in respect of the standard authorisation so far as those requirements relate to it.

(7) An assessed qualifying requirement is a qualifying requirement in relation to which a review assessment is carried out.

117 One or more review assessments negative

117 (1) This paragraph applies if one or more of the review assessments carried out comes to a negative conclusion.

(2) The supervisory body must terminate the standard authorisation with immediate effect.

118 Completion of a review

118 (1) The review of the standard authorisation is complete in any of the following cases.

(2) The first case is where paragraph 110 applies.

(3) The second case is where—
- (a) paragraph 111 applies, and
- (b) paragraph 117 requires the supervisory body to terminate the standard authorisation.

(4) In such a case, the supervisory body need not comply with any of the other provisions of paragraphs 114 to 116 which would be applicable to the review (were it not for this sub-paragraph).

(5) The third case is where—

(a) paragraph 111 applies,

(b) paragraph 117 does not require the supervisory body to terminate the standard authorisation, and

(c) the supervisory body comply with all of the provisions of paragraphs 114 to 116 (so far as they are applicable to the review).

119 Variations under this Part

119 Any variation of the standard authorisation made under this Part must be in writing.

120 Notice of outcome of review

120 (1) When the review of the standard authorisation is complete, the supervisory body must give notice to all of the following—

(a) the managing authority of the relevant hospital or care home;

(b) the relevant person;

(c) the relevant person's representative;

(d) any section 39D IMCA.

(2) That notice must state—

(a) the outcome of the review, and

(b) what variation (if any) has been made to the authorisation under this Part.

121 Records

121 A supervisory body must keep a written record of the following information—

(a) each request for a review that is made to them;

(b) the outcome of each request;

(c) each review which they carry out;

(d) the outcome of each review which they carry out;

(e) any variation of an authorisation made in consequence of a review.

122 Relationship between review and suspension under Part 6

122 (1) This paragraph applies if a standard authorisation is suspended in accordance with Part 6.

(2) No review may be requested under this Part whilst the standard authorisation is suspended.

(3) If a review has already been requested, or is being carried out, when the standard authorisation is suspended, no steps are to be taken in connection with that review whilst the authorisation is suspended.

123 Relationship between review and request for new authorisation

123 (1) This paragraph applies if, in accordance with paragraph 24 (as read with paragraph 29), the managing authority of the relevant hospital or care home make a request for a new standard authorisation which would be in force after the expiry of the existing authorisation.

(2) No review may be requested under this Part until the request for the new standard authorisation has been disposed of.

(3) If a review has already been requested, or is being carried out, when the new standard authorisation is requested, no steps are to be taken in connection with that review until the request for the new standard authorisation has been disposed of.

124 (1) This paragraph applies if—

(a) a review under this Part has been requested, or is being carried out, and

(b) the managing authority of the relevant hospital or care home make a request under paragraph 30 for a new standard authorisation which would be in force on or before, and after, the expiry of the existing authorisation.

(2) No steps are to be taken in connection with the review under this Part until the request for the new standard authorisation has been disposed of.

125 In paragraphs 123 and 124—

(a) the existing authorisation is the authorisation referred to in paragraph 101;

(b) the expiry of the existing authorisation is the time when it is expected to cease to be in force.

PART 9

ASSESSMENTS UNDER THIS SCHEDULE

126 Introduction

126 This Part contains provision about assessments under this Schedule.

127 An assessment under this Schedule is either of the following—

(a) an assessment carried out in connection with a request for a standard authorisation under Part 4;

(b) a review assessment carried out in connection with a review of a standard authorisation under Part 8.

128 In this Part, in relation to an assessment under this Schedule—

"assessor" means the person carrying out the assessment;

"relevant procedure" means—

(a) the request for the standard authorisation, or

(b) the review of the standard authorisation;

"supervisory body" means the supervisory body responsible for securing that the assessment is carried out.

129 Supervisory body to select assessor

129 (1) It is for the supervisory body to select a person to carry out an assessment under this Schedule.

(2) The supervisory body must not select a person to carry out an assessment unless the person—

(a) appears to the supervisory body to be suitable to carry out the assessment (having regard, in particular, to the type of assessment and the person to be assessed), and

(b) is eligible to carry out the assessment.

(3) Regulations may make provision about the selection, and eligibility, of persons to carry out assessments under this Schedule.

(4) Sub-paragraphs (5) and (6) apply if two or more assessments are to be obtained for the purposes of the relevant procedure.

(5) In a case where the assessments to be obtained include a mental health assessment and a best interests assessment, the supervisory body must not select the same person to carry out both assessments.

(6) Except as prohibited by sub-paragraph (5), the supervisory body may select the same person to carry out any number of the assessments which the person appears to be suitable, and is eligible, to carry out.

130 (1) This paragraph applies to regulations under paragraph 129(3).

(2) The regulations may make provision relating to a person's—

(a) qualifications,

(b) skills,

(c) training,

(d) experience,

(e) relationship to, or connection with, the relevant person or any other person,

(f) involvement in the care or treatment of the relevant person,

(g) connection with the supervisory body, or

(h) connection with the relevant hospital or care home, or with any other establishment or undertaking.

(3) The provision that the regulations may make in relation to a person's training may provide for particular training to be specified by the appropriate authority otherwise than in the regulations.

(4) In sub-paragraph (3) the "appropriate authority" means—

(a) in relation to England: the Secretary of State;

(b) in relation to Wales: the National Assembly for Wales.

(5) The regulations may make provision requiring a person to be insured in respect of liabilities that may arise in connection with the carrying out of an assessment.

(6) In relation to cases where two or more assessments are to be obtained for the purposes of the relevant procedure, the regulations may limit the number, kind or combination of assessments which a particular person is eligible to carry out.

(7) Sub-paragraphs (2) to (6) do not limit the generality of the provision that may be made in the regulations.

131 Examination and copying of records

131 An assessor may, at all reasonable times, examine and take copies of—

(a) any health record,

(b) any record of, or held by, a local authority and compiled in accordance with a social services function, and

(c) any record held by a person registered under Part 2 of the Care Standards Act 2000,

which the assessor considers may be relevant to the assessment which is being carried out.

132 Representations

132 In carrying out an assessment under this Schedule, the assessor must take into account any information given, or submissions made, by any of the following—

(a) the relevant person's representative;

(b) any section 39A IMCA;

(c) any section 39C IMCA;

(d) any section 39D IMCA.

133 Assessments to stop if any comes to negative conclusion

133 (1) This paragraph applies if an assessment under this Schedule comes to the conclusion that the relevant person does not meet one of the qualifying requirements.

(2) This Schedule does not require the supervisory body to secure that any other assessments under this Schedule are carried out in relation to the relevant procedure.

(3) The supervisory body must give notice to any assessor who is carrying out another assessment in connection with the relevant procedure that they are to cease carrying out that assessment.

(4) If an assessor receives such notice, this Schedule does not require the assessor to continue carrying out that assessment.

134 Duty to keep records and give copies

134 (1) This paragraph applies if an assessor has carried out an assessment under this Schedule (whatever conclusions the assessment has come to).

(2) The assessor must keep a written record of the assessment.

(3) As soon as practicable after carrying out the assessment, the assessor must give copies of the assessment to the supervisory body.

135 (1) This paragraph applies to the supervisory body if they are given a copy of an assessment under this Schedule.

(2) The supervisory body must give copies of the assessment to all of the following—

(a) the managing authority of the relevant hospital or care home;

(b) the relevant person;

(c) any section 39A IMCA;

(d) the relevant person's representative.

(3) If—

(a) the assessment is obtained in relation to a request for a standard authorisation, and

(b) the supervisory body are required by paragraph 50(1) to give the standard authorisation,

the supervisory body must give the copies of the assessment when they give copies of the authorisation in accordance with paragraph 57.

(4) If—

(a) the assessment is obtained in relation to a request for a standard authorisation, and

(b) the supervisory body are prohibited by paragraph 50(2) from giving the standard authorisation,

the supervisory body must give the copies of the assessment when they give notice in accordance with paragraph 58.

(5) If the assessment is obtained in connection with the review of a standard authorisation, the supervisory body must give the copies of the assessment when they give notice in accordance with paragraph 120.

136 (1) This paragraph applies to the supervisory body if—

(a) they are given a copy of a best interests assessment, and

(b) the assessment includes, in accordance with paragraph 44(2), a statement that it appears to the assessor that there is an unauthorised deprivation of liberty.

(2) The supervisory body must notify all of the persons listed in sub-paragraph (3) that the assessment includes such a statement.

(3) Those persons are—

(a) the managing authority of the relevant hospital or care home;

(b) the relevant person;

(c) any section 39A IMCA;

(d) any interested person consulted by the best interests assessor.

(4) The supervisory body must comply with this paragraph when (or at some time before) they comply with paragraph 135.

PART 10

RELEVANT PERSON'S REPRESENTATIVE

137 The representative

137 In this Schedule the relevant person's representative is the person appointed as such in accordance with this Part.

138 (1) Regulations may make provision about the selection and appointment of representatives.

(2) In this Part such regulations are referred to as "appointment regulations".

139 Supervisory body to appoint representative

139 (1) The supervisory body must appoint a person to be the relevant person's representative as soon as practicable after a standard authorisation is given.

(2) The supervisory body must appoint a person to be the relevant person's representative if a vacancy arises whilst a standard authorisation is in force.

(3) Where a vacancy arises, the appointment under sub-paragraph (2) is to be made as soon as practicable after the supervisory body becomes aware of the vacancy.

140 (1) The selection of a person for appointment under paragraph 139 must not be made unless it appears to the person making the selection that the prospective representative would, if appointed—

(a) maintain contact with the relevant person,

(b) represent the relevant person in matters relating to or connected with this Schedule, and

(c) support the relevant person in matters relating to or connected with this Schedule.

141 (1) Any appointment of a representative for a relevant person is in addition to, and does not affect, any appointment of a donee or deputy.

(2) The functions of any representative are in addition to, and do not affect—

(a) the authority of any donee,

(b) the powers of any deputy, or

(c) any powers of the court.

142 Appointment regulations

142 Appointment regulations may provide that the procedure for appointing a representative may begin at any time after a request for a standard authorisation is made (including a time before the request has been disposed of).

143 (1) Appointment regulations may make provision about who is to select a person for appointment as a representative.

(2) But regulations under this paragraph may only provide for the following to make a selection—

(a) the relevant person, if he has capacity in relation to the question of which person should be his representative;

(b) a donee of a lasting power of attorney granted by the relevant person, if it is within the scope of his authority to select a person;

(c) a deputy, if it is within the scope of his authority to select a person;

(d) a best interests assessor;

(e) the supervisory body.

(3) Regulations under this paragraph may provide that a selection by the relevant person, a donee or a deputy is subject to approval by a best interests assessor or the supervisory body.

(4) Regulations under this paragraph may provide that, if more than one selection is necessary in connection with the appointment of a particular representative—

(a) the same person may make more than one selection;

(b) different persons may make different selections.

(5) For the purposes of this paragraph a best interests assessor is a person carrying out a best interests assessment in connection with the standard authorisation in question (including the giving of that authorisation).

144 (1) Appointment regulations may make provision about who may, or may not, be—

(a) selected for appointment as a representative, or

(b) appointed as a representative.

(2) Regulations under this paragraph may relate to any of the following matters—

(a) a person's age;

(b) a person's suitability;

(c) a person's independence;

(d) a person's willingness;

(e) a person's qualifications.

145 Appointment regulations may make provision about the formalities of appointing a person as a representative.

146 In a case where a best interests assessor is to select a person to be appointed as a representative, appointment regulations may provide for the variation of the assessor's duties in relation to the assessment which he is carrying out.

147 Monitoring of representatives

147 Regulations may make provision requiring the managing authority of the relevant hospital or care home to—

(a) monitor, and

(b) report to the supervisory body on,

the extent to which a representative is maintaining contact with the relevant person.

148 Termination

148 Regulations may make provision about the circumstances in which the appointment of a person as the relevant person's representative ends or may be ended.

149 Regulations may make provision about the formalities of ending the appointment of a person as a representative.

150 Suspension of representative's functions

150 (1) Regulations may make provision about the circumstances in which functions exercisable by, or in relation to, the relevant person's representative (whether under this Schedule or not) may be—

(a) suspended, and

(b) if suspended, revived.

(2) The regulations may make provision about the formalities for giving effect to the suspension or revival of a function.

(3) The regulations may make provision about the effect of the suspension or revival of a function.

151 Payment of representative

151 Regulations may make provision for payments to be made to, or in relation to, persons exercising functions as the relevant person's representative.

152 Regulations under this Part

152 The provisions of this Part which specify provision that may be made in regulations under this Part do not affect the generality of the power to make such regulations.

153 Effect of appointment of section 39C IMCA

153 Paragraphs 159 and 160 make provision about the exercise of functions by, or towards, the relevant person's representative during periods when—

(a) no person is appointed as the relevant person's representative, but

(b) a person is appointed as a section 39C IMCA.

PART 11

IMCAs

154 Application of Part

154 This Part applies for the purposes of this Schedule.

155 The IMCAs

155 A section 39A IMCA is an independent mental capacity advocate appointed under section 39A.

156 A section 39C IMCA is an independent mental capacity advocate appointed under section 39C.

157 A section 39D IMCA is an independent mental capacity advocate appointed under section 39D.

158 An IMCA is a section 39A IMCA or a section 39C IMCA or a section 39D IMCA.

159 Section 39C IMCA: functions

159 (1) This paragraph applies if, and for as long as, there is a section 39C IMCA.

(2) In the application of the relevant provisions, references to the relevant person's representative are to be read as references to the section 39C IMCA.

(3) But sub-paragraph (2) does not apply to any function under the relevant provisions for as long as the function is suspended in accordance with provision made under Part 10.

(4) In this paragraph and paragraph 160 the relevant provisions are—

(a) paragraph 102(3)(b) (request for review under Part 8);

(b) paragraph 108(1)(b) (notice of review under Part 8);

(c) paragraph 120(1)(c) (notice of outcome of review under Part 8).

160 (1) This paragraph applies if—
(a) a person is appointed as the relevant person's representative, and
(b) a person accordingly ceases to hold an appointment as a section 39C IMCA.

(2) Where a function under a relevant provision has been exercised by, or towards, the section 39C IMCA, there is no requirement for that function to be exercised again by, or towards, the relevant person's representative.

161 Section 39A IMCA: restriction of functions

161 (1) This paragraph applies if—
(a) there is a section 39A IMCA, and
(b) a person is appointed under Part 10 to be the relevant person's representative (whether or not that person, or any person subsequently appointed, is currently the relevant person's representative).

(2) The duties imposed on, and the powers exercisable by, the section 39A IMCA do not apply.

(3) The duties imposed on, and the powers exercisable by, any other person do not apply, so far as they fall to be performed or exercised towards the section 39A IMCA.

(4) But sub-paragraph (2) does not apply to any power of challenge exercisable by the section 39A IMCA.

(5) And sub-paragraph (3) does not apply to any duty or power of any other person so far as it relates to any power of challenge exercisable by the section 39A IMCA.

(6) Before exercising any power of challenge, the section 39A IMCA must take the views of the relevant person's representative into account.

(7) A power of challenge is a power to make an application to the court to exercise its jurisdiction under section 21A in connection with the giving of the standard authorisation.

PART 12

MISCELLANEOUS

162 Monitoring of operation of Schedule

162 (1) Regulations may make provision for, and in connection with, requiring one or more prescribed bodies to monitor, and report on, the operation of this Schedule in relation to England.

(2) The regulations may, in particular, give a prescribed body authority to do one or more of the following things—
(a) to visit hospitals and care homes;
(b) to visit and interview persons accommodated in hospitals and care homes;
(c) to require the production of, and to inspect, records relating to the care or treatment of persons.

(3) "Prescribed" means prescribed in regulations under this paragraph.

163 (1) Regulations may make provision for, and in connection with, enabling the National Assembly for Wales to monitor, and report on, the operation of this Schedule in relation to Wales.

(2) The National Assembly may direct one or more persons or bodies to carry out the Assembly's functions under regulations under this paragraph.

164 Disclosure of information

164 (1) Regulations may require either or both of the following to disclose prescribed information to prescribed bodies—

(a) supervisory bodies;

(b) managing authorities of hospitals or care homes.

(2) "Prescribed" means prescribed in regulations under this paragraph.

(3) Regulations under this paragraph may only prescribe information relating to matters with which this Schedule is concerned.

165 Directions by National Assembly in relation to supervisory functions

165 (1) The National Assembly for Wales may direct a Local Health Board to exercise in relation to its area any supervisory functions which are specified in the direction.

(2) Directions under this paragraph must not preclude the National Assembly from exercising the functions specified in the directions.

(3) In this paragraph "supervisory functions" means functions which the National Assembly have as supervisory body, so far as they are exercisable in relation to hospitals (whether NHS or independent hospitals, and whether in Wales or England).

166 (1) This paragraph applies where, under paragraph 165, a Local Health Board ("the specified LHB") is directed to exercise supervisory functions ("delegated functions").

(2) The National Assembly for Wales may give directions to the specified LHB about the Board's exercise of delegated functions.

(3) The National Assembly may give directions for any delegated functions to be exercised, on behalf of the specified LHB, by a committee, sub-committee or officer of that Board.

(4) The National Assembly may give directions providing for any delegated functions to be exercised by the specified LHB jointly with one or more other Local Health Boards.

(5) Where, under sub-paragraph (4), delegated functions are exercisable jointly, the National Assembly may give directions providing for the functions to be exercised, on behalf of the Local Health Boards in question, by a joint committee or joint sub-committee.

167 (1) Directions under paragraph 165 must be given in regulations.

(2) Directions under paragraph 166 may be given—

(a) in regulations, or

(b) by instrument in writing.

168 The power under paragraph 165 or paragraph 166 to give directions includes power to vary or revoke directions given under that paragraph.

169 Notices

169 Any notice under this Schedule must be in writing.

170 Regulations

170 (1) This paragraph applies to all regulations under this Schedule, except regulations under paragraph 162, 163, 167 or 183.

(2) It is for the Secretary of State to make such regulations in relation to authorisations under this Schedule which relate to hospitals and care homes situated in England.

(3) It is for the National Assembly for Wales to make such regulations in relation to authorisations under this Schedule which relate to hospitals and care homes situated in Wales.

171 It is for the Secretary of State to make regulations under paragraph 162.

172 It is for the National Assembly for Wales to make regulations under paragraph 163 or 167.

173 (1) This paragraph applies to regulations under paragraph 183.

(2) It is for the Secretary of State to make such regulations in relation to cases where a question as to the ordinary residence of a person is to be determined by the Secretary of State.

(3) It is for the National Assembly for Wales to make such regulations in relation to cases where a question as to the ordinary residence of a person is to be determined by the National Assembly.

PART 13

INTERPRETATION

174 Introduction

174 This Part applies for the purposes of this Schedule.

175 Hospitals and their managing authorities

175 (1) "Hospital" means—

(a) an NHS hospital, or
(b) an independent hospital.

(2) "NHS hospital" means—

(a) a health service hospital as defined by section 275 of the National Health Service Act 2006 or section 206 of the National Health Service (Wales) Act 2006, or

(b) a hospital as defined by section 206 of the National Health Service (Wales) Act 2006 vested in a Local Health Board.

(3) "Independent hospital" means a hospital as defined by section 2 of the Care Standards Act 2000 which is not an NHS hospital.

176 (1) "Managing authority", in relation to an NHS hospital, means—

(a) if the hospital—

(i) is vested in the appropriate national authority for the purposes of its functions under the National Health Service Act 2006 or of the National Health Service (Wales) Act 2006, or

(ii) consists of any accommodation provided by a local authority and used as a hospital by or on behalf of the appropriate national authority under either of those Acts,

the Primary Care Trust, Strategic Health Authority, Local Health Board or Special Health Authority responsible for the administration of the hospital;

(b) if the hospital is vested in a Primary Care Trust, National Health Service trust or NHS foundation trust, that trust;

(c) if the hospital is vested in a Local Health Board, that Board.

(2) For this purpose the appropriate national authority is—

(a) in relation to England: the Secretary of State;

(b) in relation to Wales: the National Assembly for Wales;

(c) in relation to England and Wales: the Secretary of State and the National Assembly acting jointly.

177 "Managing authority", in relation to an independent hospital, means the person registered, or required to be registered, under Part 2 of the Care Standards Act 2000 in respect of the hospital.

178 Care homes and their managing authorities

178 "Care home" has the meaning given by section 3 of the Care Standards Act 2000.

179 "Managing authority", in relation to a care home, means the person registered, or required to be registered, under Part 2 of the Care Standards Act 2000 in respect of the care home.

180 Supervisory bodies: hospitals

180 (1) The identity of the supervisory body is determined under this paragraph in cases where the relevant hospital is situated in England.

(2) If a Primary Care Trust commissions the relevant care or treatment, that Trust is the supervisory body.

(3) If the National Assembly for Wales or a Local Health Board commission the relevant care or treatment, the National Assembly are the supervisory body.

(4) In any other case, the supervisory body are the Primary Care Trust for the area in which the relevant hospital is situated.

(5) If a hospital is situated in the areas of two (or more) Primary Care Trusts, it is to be regarded for the purposes of sub-paragraph (4) as situated in whichever of the areas the greater (or greatest) part of the hospital is situated.

181 (1) The identity of the supervisory body is determined under this paragraph in cases where the relevant hospital is situated in Wales.

(2) The National Assembly for Wales are the supervisory body.

(3) But if a Primary Care Trust commissions the relevant care or treatment, that Trust is the supervisory body.

182 Supervisory bodies: care homes

182 (1) The identity of the supervisory body is determined under this paragraph in cases where the relevant care home is situated in England or in Wales.

(2) The supervisory body are the local authority for the area in which the relevant person is ordinarily resident.

(3) But if the relevant person is not ordinarily resident in the area of a local authority, the supervisory body are the local authority for the area in which the care home is situated.

(4) In relation to England "local authority" means—

(a) the council of a county;

(b) the council of a district for which there is no county council;

(c) the council of a London borough;

(d) the Common Council of the City of London;

(e) the Council of the Isles of Scilly.

(5) In relation to Wales "local authority" means the council of a county or county borough.

(6) If a care home is situated in the areas of two (or more) local authorities, it is to be regarded for the purposes of sub-paragraph (3) as situated in whichever of the areas the greater (or greatest) part of the care home is situated.

183 (1) Subsections (5) and (6) of section 24 of the National Assistance Act 1948 (deemed place of ordinary residence) apply to any determination of where a person is ordinarily resident for the purposes of paragraph 182 as those subsections apply to such a determination for the purposes specified in those subsections.

(2) In the application of section 24(6) of the 1948 Act by virtue of sub-paragraph (1), section 24(6) is to be read as if it referred to a hospital vested in a Local Health Board as well as to hospitals vested in the Secretary of State and the other bodies mentioned in section 24(6).

(3) Any question arising as to the ordinary residence of a person is to be determined by the Secretary of State or by the National Assembly for Wales.

(4) The Secretary of State and the National Assembly must make and publish arrangements for determining which cases are to be dealt with by the Secretary of State and which are to be dealt with by the National Assembly.

(5) Those arrangements may include provision for the Secretary of State and the National Assembly to agree, in relation to any question that has arisen, which of them is to deal with the case.

(6) Regulations may make provision about arrangements that are to have effect before, upon, or after the determination of any question as to the ordinary residence of a person.

(7) The regulations may, in particular, authorise or require a local authority to do any or all of the following things—

(a) to act as supervisory body even though it may wish to dispute that it is the supervisory body;

(b) to become the supervisory body in place of another local authority;

(c) to recover from another local authority expenditure incurred in exercising functions as the supervisory body.

184 Same body managing authority and supervisory body

184 (1) This paragraph applies if, in connection with a particular person's detention as a resident in a hospital or care home, the same body are both—

(a) the managing authority of the relevant hospital or care home, and

(b) the supervisory body.

(2) The fact that a single body are acting in both capacities does not prevent the body from carrying out functions under this Schedule in each capacity.

(3) But, in such a case, this Schedule has effect subject to any modifications contained in regulations that may be made for this purpose.

185 Interested persons

185 Each of the following is an interested person—

(a) the relevant person's spouse or civil partner;

(b) where the relevant person and another person of the opposite sex are not married to each other but are living together as husband and wife: the other person;

(c) where the relevant person and another person of the same sex are not civil partners of each other but are living together as if they were civil partners: the other person;

(d) the relevant person's children and step-children;

(e) the relevant person's parents and step-parents;

(f) the relevant person's brothers and sisters, half-brothers and half-sisters, and stepbrothers and stepsisters;

(g) the relevant person's grandparents;

(h) a deputy appointed for the relevant person by the court;

(i) a donee of a lasting power of attorney granted by the relevant person.

186 (1) An interested person consulted by the best interests assessor is any person whose name is stated in the relevant best interests assessment in accordance with paragraph 40 (interested persons whom the assessor consulted in carrying out the assessment).

(2) The relevant best interests assessment is the most recent best interests assessment carried out in connection with the standard authorisation in question (whether the assessment was carried out under Part 4 or Part 8).

187 Where this Schedule imposes on a person a duty towards an interested person, the duty does not apply if the person on whom the duty is imposed—

(a) is not aware of the interested person's identity or of a way of contacting him, and

(b) cannot reasonably ascertain it.

188 The following table contains an index of provisions defining or otherwise explaining expressions used in this Schedule—

age assessment	paragraph 34
age requirement	paragraph 13
age review assessment	paragraph 112(3)
appointment regulations	paragraph 138
assessment under this Schedule	paragraph 127
assessor (except in Part 9)	paragraph 33
assessor (in Part 9)	paragraphs 33 and 128
authorisation under this Schedule	paragraph 10
best interests (determination of)	section 4
best interests assessment	paragraph 38
best interests requirement	paragraph 16
best interests review assessment	paragraph 112(6)
care home	paragraph 178
change of reason ground	paragraph 106
complete (in relation to a review of a standard authorisation)	paragraph 118
deprivation of a person's liberty	section 64(5) and (6)
deputy	section 16(2)(b)
detained resident	paragraph 6
disposed of (in relation to a request for a standard authorisation)	paragraph 66
eligibility assessment	paragraph 46
eligibility requirement	paragraph 17
eligibility review assessment	paragraph 112(7)
eligible person (in relation to paragraphs 68 to 73)	paragraph 68
eligible person (in relation to Part 8)	paragraph 102(3)
expiry (in relation to an existing authorisation)	paragraph 125(b)
existing authorisation (in Part 8)	paragraph 125(a)

hospital	paragraph 175
IMCA	paragraph 158
in force (in relation to a standard authorisation)	paragraphs 63 and 64
in force (in relation to an urgent authorisation)	paragraphs 88 and 89
ineligible (in relation to the eligibility requirement)	Schedule 1A
interested person	paragraph 185
interested person consulted by the best interests assessor	paragraph 186
lack of capacity	section 2
lasting power of attorney	section 9
managing authority (in relation to a care home)	paragraph 179
managing authority (in relation to a hospital)	paragraph 176 or 177
maximum authorisation period	paragraph 42
mental capacity assessment	paragraph 37
mental capacity requirement	paragraph 15
mental capacity review assessment	paragraph 112(5)
mental health assessment	paragraph 35
mental health requirement	paragraph 14
mental health review assessment	paragraph 112(4)
negative conclusion	paragraph 112(2)(a)
new supervisory body	paragraph 99(b)
no refusals assessment	paragraph 48
no refusals requirement	paragraph 18
no refusals review assessment	paragraph 112(8)
non-qualification ground	paragraph 105
old supervisory body	paragraph 99(a)
positive conclusion	paragraph 112(2)(b)
purpose of a standard authorisation	paragraph 11(1)
purpose of an urgent authorisation	paragraph 11(2)
qualifying requirements	paragraph 12
refusal (for the purposes of the no refusals requirement)	paragraphs 19 and 20

relevant care or treatment	paragraph 7
relevant hospital or care home	paragraph 7
relevant managing authority	paragraph 26(4)
relevant person	paragraph 7
relevant person's representative	paragraph 137
relevant procedure	paragraph 128
review assessment	paragraph 112(1)
reviewable	paragraph 104
section 39A IMCA	paragraph 155
section 39C IMCA	paragraph 156
section 39D IMCA	paragraph 157
standard authorisation	paragraph 8
supervisory body (except in Part 9)	paragraph 180, 181 or 182
supervisory body (in Part 9)	paragraph 128 and paragraph 180, 181 or 182
unauthorised deprivation of liberty (in relation to paragraphs 68 to 73)	paragraph 67
urgent authorisation	paragraph 9
variation of conditions ground	paragraph 107".

SCHEDULE 8

Section 50

MENTAL CAPACITY ACT 2005: NEW SCHEDULE 1A

After Schedule 1 to the Mental Capacity Act 2005 (c. 9) insert—

"SCHEDULE 1A

PERSONS INELIGIBLE TO BE DEPRIVED OF LIBERTY BY THIS ACT

PART 1

INELIGIBLE PERSONS

1 Application

1 This Schedule applies for the purposes of—

(a) section 16A, and

(b) paragraph 17 of Schedule A1.

2 Determining ineligibility

2 A person ("P") is ineligible to be deprived of liberty by this Act ("ineligible") if—

(a) P falls within one of the cases set out in the second column of the following table, and

(b) the corresponding entry in the third column of the table —or the provision, or one of the provisions, referred to in that entry — provides that he is ineligible.

	Status of P	*Determination of ineligibility*
Case A	P is— (a) subject to the hospital treatment regime, and (b) detained in a hospital under that regime.	P is ineligible.
Case B	P is— (a) subject to the hospital treatment regime, but (b) not detained in a hospital under that regime.	See paragraphs 3 and 4.
Case C	P is subject to the community treatment regime.	See paragraphs 3 and 4.
Case D	P is subject to the guardianship regime.	See paragraphs 3 and 5.
Case E	P is— (a) within the scope of the Mental Health Act, but (b) not subject to any of the mental health regimes.	See paragraph 5.

3 Authorised course of action not in accordance with regime

3 (1) This paragraph applies in cases B, C and D in the table in paragraph 2.

(2) P is ineligible if the authorised course of action is not in accordance with a requirement which the relevant regime imposes.

(3) That includes any requirement as to where P is, or is not, to reside.

(4) The relevant regime is the mental health regime to which P is subject.

4 Treatment for mental disorder in a hospital

4 (1) This paragraph applies in cases B and C in the table in paragraph 2.

(2) P is ineligible if the relevant care or treatment consists in whole or in part of medical treatment for mental disorder in a hospital.

5 P objects to being a mental health patient etc

5 (1) This paragraph applies in cases D and E in the table in paragraph 2.

(2) P is ineligible if the following conditions are met.

(3) The first condition is that the relevant instrument authorises P to be a mental health patient.

(4) The second condition is that P objects—

(a) to being a mental health patient, or

(b) to being given some or all of the mental health treatment.

(5) The third condition is that a donee or deputy has not made a valid decision to consent to each matter to which P objects.

(6) In determining whether or not P objects to something, regard must be had to all the circumstances (so far as they are reasonably ascertainable), including the following—

(a) P's behaviour;

(b) P's wishes and feelings;

(c) P's views, beliefs and values.

(7) But regard is to be had to circumstances from the past only so far as it is still appropriate to have regard to them.

PART 2

INTERPRETATION

6 Application

6 This Part applies for the purposes of this Schedule.

7 Mental health regimes

7 The mental health regimes are—

(a) the hospital treatment regime,

(b) the community treatment regime, and

(c) the guardianship regime.

8 Hospital treatment regime

8 (1) P is subject to the hospital treatment regime if he is subject to—

(a) a hospital treatment obligation under the relevant enactment, or

(b) an obligation under another England and Wales enactment which has the same effect as a hospital treatment obligation.

(2) But where P is subject to any such obligation, he is to be regarded as not subject to the hospital treatment regime during any period when he is subject to the community treatment regime.

(3) A hospital treatment obligation is an application, order or direction of a kind listed in the first column of the following table.

(4) In relation to a hospital treatment obligation, the relevant enactment is the enactment in the Mental Health Act which is referred to in the corresponding entry in the second column of the following table.

Hospital treatment obligation	*Relevant enactment*
Application for admission for assessment	Section 2
Application for admission for assessment	Section 4
Application for admission for treatment	Section 3
Order for remand to hospital	Section 35
Order for remand to hospital	Section 36
Hospital order	Section 37
Interim hospital order	Section 38
Order for detention in hospital	Section 44
Hospital direction	Section 45A
Transfer direction	Section 47
Transfer direction	Section 48
Hospital order	Section 51

9 Community treatment regime

9 P is subject to the community treatment regime if he is subject to—

(a) a community treatment order under section 17A of the Mental Health Act, or

(b) an obligation under another England and Wales enactment which has the same effect as a community treatment order.

10 Guardianship regime

10 P is subject to the guardianship regime if he is subject to—

(a) a guardianship application under section 7 of the Mental Health Act,

(b) a guardianship order under section 37 of the Mental Health Act, or

(c) an obligation under another England and Wales enactment which has the same effect as a guardianship application or guardianship order.

11 England and Wales enactments

11 (1) An England and Wales enactment is an enactment which extends to England and Wales (whether or not it also extends elsewhere).

(2) It does not matter if the enactment is in the Mental Health Act or not.

12 P within scope of Mental Health Act

12 (1) P is within the scope of the Mental Health Act if—

(a) an application in respect of P could be made under section 2 or 3 of the Mental Health Act, and

(b) P could be detained in a hospital in pursuance of such an application, were one made.

(2) The following provisions of this paragraph apply when determining whether an application in respect of P could be made under section 2 or 3 of the Mental Health Act.

(3) If the grounds in section 2(2) of the Mental Health Act are met in P's case, it is to be assumed that the recommendations referred to in section 2(3) of that Act have been given.

(4) If the grounds in section 3(2) of the Mental Health Act are met in P's case, it is to be assumed that the recommendations referred to in section 3(3) of that Act have been given.

(5) In determining whether the ground in section 3(2)(c) of the Mental Health Act is met in P's case, it is to be assumed that the treatment referred to in section 3(2)(c) cannot be provided under this Act.

13 Authorised course of action, relevant care or treatment & relevant instrument

13 In a case where this Schedule applies for the purposes of section 16A—

"authorised course of action" means any course of action amounting to deprivation of liberty which the order under section 16(2)(a) authorises;

"relevant care or treatment" means any care or treatment which—

(a) comprises, or forms part of, the authorised course of action, or

(b) is to be given in connection with the authorised course of action;

"relevant instrument" means the order under section 16(2)(a).

14 In a case where this Schedule applies for the purposes of paragraph 17 of Schedule A1—

"authorised course of action" means the accommodation of the relevant person in the relevant hospital or care home for the purpose of being given the relevant care or treatment;

"relevant care or treatment" has the same meaning as in Schedule A1;

"relevant instrument" means the standard authorisation under Schedule A1.

15 (1) This paragraph applies where the question whether a person is ineligible to be deprived of liberty by this Act is relevant to either of these decisions—

(a) whether or not to include particular provision ("the proposed provision") in an order under section 16(2)(a);

(b) whether or not to give a standard authorisation under Schedule A1.

(2) A reference in this Schedule to the authorised course of action or the relevant care or treatment is to be read as a reference to that thing as it would be if—

(a) the proposed provision were included in the order, or

(b) the standard authorisation were given.

(3) A reference in this Schedule to the relevant instrument is to be read as follows—

(a) where the relevant instrument is an order under section 16(2)(a): as a reference to the order as it would be if the proposed provision were included in it;

(b) where the relevant instrument is a standard authorisation: as a reference to the standard authorisation as it would be if it were given.

16 Expressions used in paragraph 5

16 (1) These expressions have the meanings given—

"donee" means a donee of a lasting power of attorney granted by P;

"mental health patient" means a person accommodated in a hospital for the purpose of being given medical treatment for mental disorder;

"mental health treatment" means the medical treatment for mental disorder referred to in the definition of "mental health patient".

(2) A decision of a donee or deputy is valid if it is made—

(a) within the scope of his authority as donee or deputy, and

(b) in accordance with Part 1 of this Act.

17 Expressions with same meaning as in Mental Health Act

17 (1) "Hospital" has the same meaning as in Part 2 of the Mental Health Act.

(2) "Medical treatment" has the same meaning as in the Mental Health Act.

(3) "Mental disorder" has the same meaning as in Schedule A1 (see paragraph 14).".

SCHEDULE 9

Section 50

AMENDMENTS RELATING TO NEW SECTION 4A OF, & SCHEDULE A1 TO, MENTAL CAPACITY ACT 2005

PART 1

OTHER AMENDMENTS TO MENTAL CAPACITY ACT 2005

Introduction

1 The Mental Capacity Act 2005 (c. 9) is amended as set out in this Part of this Schedule.

New section 21A

2 After section 21 insert—

"Powers of the court in relation to Schedule A1

21A Powers of court in relation to Schedule A1

21A Powers of court in relation to Schedule A1

(1) This section applies if either of the following has been given under Schedule A1—

(a) a standard authorisation;

(b) an urgent authorisation.

(2) Where a standard authorisation has been given, the court may determine any question relating to any of the following matters—

(a) whether the relevant person meets one or more of the qualifying requirements;

(b) the period during which the standard authorisation is to be in force;

(c) the purpose for which the standard authorisation is given;

(d) the conditions subject to which the standard authorisation is given.

(3) If the court determines any question under subsection (2), the court may make an order—

(a) varying or terminating the standard authorisation, or

(b) directing the supervisory body to vary or terminate the standard authorisation.

(4) Where an urgent authorisation has been given, the court may determine any question relating to any of the following matters—

(a) whether the urgent authorisation should have been given;

(b) the period during which the urgent authorisation is to be in force;

(c) the purpose for which the urgent authorisation is given.

(5) Where the court determines any question under subsection (4), the court may make an order—

(a) varying or terminating the urgent authorisation, or

(b) directing the managing authority of the relevant hospital or care home to vary or terminate the urgent authorisation.

(6) Where the court makes an order under subsection (3) or (5), the court may make an order about a person's liability for any act done in connection with the standard or urgent authorisation before its variation or termination.

(7) An order under subsection (6) may, in particular, exclude a person from liability."

Section 35: Appointment of independent mental capacity advocates

3 In section 35, in subsection (1) after "relate" insert "or persons who fall within section 39A, 39C or 39D".

Section 38: IMCAs and provision of accommodation by NHS body

4 (1) Section 38 is amended as follows.

(2) After subsection (2) insert—

"(2A) And this section does not apply if—

(a) an independent mental capacity advocate must be appointed under section 39A or 39C (whether or not by the NHS body) to represent P, and

(b) the hospital or care home in which P is to be accommodated under the arrangements referred to in this section is the relevant hospital or care home under the authorisation referred to in that section."

(3) After subsection (9) insert—

"(10) For the purposes of subsection (1), a person appointed under Part 10 of Schedule A1 to be P's representative is not, by virtue of that appointment, engaged in providing care or treatment for P in a professional capacity or for remuneration."

Section 39: IMCAs and provision of accommodation by local authority

5 (1) Section 39 is amended as follows.

(2) After subsection (3) insert—

"(3A) And this section does not apply if—

(a) an independent mental capacity advocate must be appointed under section 39A or 39C (whether or not by the local authority) to represent P, and

(b) the place in which P is to be accommodated under the arrangements referred to in this section is the relevant hospital or care home under the authorisation referred to in that section."

(3) After subsection (6) insert—

"(7) For the purposes of subsection (1), a person appointed under Part 10 of Schedule A1 to be P's representative is not, by virtue of that appointment, engaged in providing care or treatment for P in a professional capacity or for remuneration."

New section 39A

6 After section 39 insert—

"39A Person becomes subject to Schedule A1

"39A Person becomes subject to Schedule A1

(1) This section applies if—

(a) a person ("P") becomes subject to Schedule A1, and

(b) the managing authority of the relevant hospital or care home are satisfied that there is no person, other than one engaged in providing care or treatment for P in a professional capacity or for remuneration, whom it would be appropriate to consult in determining what would be in P's best interests.

(2) The managing authority must notify the supervisory body that this section applies.

(3) The supervisory body must instruct an independent mental capacity advocate to represent P.

(4) Schedule A1 makes provision about the role of an independent mental capacity advocate appointed under this section.

(5) This section is subject to paragraph 161 of Schedule A1.

(6) For the purposes of subsection (1), a person appointed under Part 10 of Schedule A1 to be P's representative is not, by virtue of that appointment, engaged in providing care or treatment for P in a professional capacity or for remuneration.

39B Section 39A: supplementary provision

39B Section 39A: supplementary provision

(1) This section applies for the purposes of section 39A.

(2) P becomes subject to Schedule A1 in any of the following cases.

(3) The first case is where an urgent authorisation is given in relation to P under paragraph 76(2) of Schedule A1 (urgent authorisation given before request made for standard authorisation).

(4) The second case is where the following conditions are met.

(5) The first condition is that a request is made under Schedule A1 for a standard authorisation to be given in relation to P ("the requested authorisation").

(6) The second condition is that no urgent authorisation was given under paragraph 76(2) of Schedule A1 before that request was made.

(7) The third condition is that the requested authorisation will not be in force on or before, or immediately after, the expiry of an existing standard authorisation.

(8) The expiry of a standard authorisation is the date when the authorisation is expected to cease to be in force.

(9) The third case is where, under paragraph 69 of Schedule A1, the supervisory body select a person to carry out an assessment of whether or not the relevant person is a detained resident.

39C Person unrepresented whilst subject to Schedule A1

39C Person unrepresented whilst subject to Schedule A1

(1) This section applies if—

(a) an authorisation under Schedule A1 is in force in relation to a person ("P"),

(b) the appointment of a person as P's representative ends in accordance with regulations made under Part 10 of Schedule A1, and

(c) the managing authority of the relevant hospital or care home are satisfied that there is no person, other than one engaged in providing care or treatment for P in a professional capacity or for remuneration, whom it would be appropriate to consult in determining what would be in P's best interests.

(2) The managing authority must notify the supervisory body that this section applies.

(3) The supervisory body must instruct an independent mental capacity advocate to represent P.

(4) Paragraph 159 of Schedule A1 makes provision about the role of an independent mental capacity advocate appointed under this section.

(5) The appointment of an independent mental capacity advocate under this section ends when a new appointment of a person as P's representative is made in accordance with Part 10 of Schedule A1.

(6) For the purposes of subsection (1), a person appointed under Part 10 of Schedule A1 to be P's representative is not, by virtue of that appointment, engaged in providing care or treatment for P in a professional capacity or for remuneration.

39D Person subject to Schedule A1 without paid representative

39D Person subject to Schedule A1 without paid representative

(1) This section applies if—

(a) an authorisation under Schedule A1 is in force in relation to a person ("P"),

(b) P has a representative ("R") appointed under Part 10 of Schedule A1, and

(c) R is not being paid under regulations under Part 10 of Schedule A1 for acting as P's representative.

(2) The supervisory body must instruct an independent mental capacity advocate to represent P in any of the following cases.

(3) The first case is where P makes a request to the supervisory body to instruct an advocate.

(4) The second case is where R makes a request to the supervisory body to instruct an advocate.

(5) The third case is where the supervisory body have reason to believe one or more of the following—

(a) that, without the help of an advocate, P and R would be unable to exercise one or both of the relevant rights;

(b) that P and R have each failed to exercise a relevant right when it would have been reasonable to exercise it;

(c) that P and R are each unlikely to exercise a relevant right when it would be reasonable to exercise it.

(6) The duty in subsection (2) is subject to section 39E.

(7) If an advocate is appointed under this section, the advocate is, in particular, to take such steps as are practicable to help P and R to understand the following matters—

(a) the effect of the authorisation;

(b) the purpose of the authorisation;

(c) the duration of the authorisation;

(d) any conditions to which the authorisation is subject;

(e) the reasons why each assessor who carried out an assessment in connection with the request for the authorisation, or in connection with a review of the authorisation, decided that P met the qualifying requirement in question;

(f) the relevant rights;

(g) how to exercise the relevant rights.

(8) The advocate is, in particular, to take such steps as are practicable to help P or R—

(a) to exercise the right to apply to court, if it appears to the advocate that P or R wishes to exercise that right, or

(b) to exercise the right of review, if it appears to the advocate that P or R wishes to exercise that right.

(9) If the advocate helps P or R to exercise the right of review—

(a) the advocate may make submissions to the supervisory body on the question of whether a qualifying requirement is reviewable;

(b) the advocate may give information, or make submissions, to any assessor carrying out a review assessment.

(10) In this section—

"relevant rights" means—

(a) the right to apply to court, and

(b) the right of review;

"right to apply to court" means the right to make an application to the court to exercise its jurisdiction under section 21A;

"right of review" means the right under Part 8 of Schedule A1 to request a review.

39E Limitation on duty to instruct advocate under section 39D

39E Limitation on duty to instruct advocate under section 39D

(1) This section applies if an advocate is already representing P in accordance with an instruction under section 39D.

(2) Section 39D(2) does not require another advocate to be instructed, unless the following conditions are met.

(3) The first condition is that the existing advocate was instructed—

(a) because of a request by R, or

(b) because the supervisory body had reason to believe one or more of the things in section 39D(5).

(4) The second condition is that the other advocate would be instructed because of a request by P."

Section 40: Exceptions to duty to appoint IMCAs

7 (1) Section 40 (as substituted by section 49 of this Act) is amended as follows.

(2) The provision of section 40 becomes subsection (1) of section 40.

(3) In subsection (1) for "or 39(4) or (5)" substitute ", 39(4) or (5), 39A(3), 39C(3) or 39D(2)".

(4) After subsection (1) insert—

"(2) A person appointed under Part 10 of Schedule A1 to be P's representative is not, by virtue of that appointment, a person nominated by P as a person to be consulted in matters to which a duty mentioned in subsection (1) relates."

Section 42: Codes of practice

8 (1) Section 42 is amended as follows.

(2) In subsection (1), after paragraph (f) insert—

"(fa) for the guidance of persons exercising functions under Schedule A1,

(fb) for the guidance of representatives appointed under Part 10 of Schedule A1,".

(3) In subsection (4), after paragraph (d) insert—

"(da) in the exercise of functions under Schedule A1,

(db) as a representative appointed under Part 10 of Schedule A1,".

Section 50: Application to the Court of Protection

9 In section 50, after subsection (1) insert—

"(1A) Nor is permission required for an application to the court under section 21A by the relevant person's representative."

Section 64: Interpretation

10 (1) Section 64 is amended as follows.

(2) In subsection (1), insert at the appropriate place—

"""authorisation under Schedule A1" means either—

(a) a standard authorisation under that Schedule, or

(b) an urgent authorisation under that Schedule."

(3) In subsection (1), in the definition of "local authority" after """local authority""" insert ", except in Schedule A1,".

(4) After subsection (4) insert—

"(5) In this Act, references to deprivation of a person's liberty have the same meaning as in Article 5(1) of the Human Rights Convention.

(6) For the purposes of such references, it does not matter whether a person is deprived of his liberty by a public authority or not."

Section 65: Rules, regulations and orders

11 (1) Section 65 is amended as follows.

(2) After subsection (4) insert—

"(4A) Subsection (2) does not apply to a statutory instrument containing regulations made by the Secretary of State under Schedule A1.

(4B) If such a statutory instrument contains regulations under paragraph 42(2)(b), 129, 162 or 164 of Schedule A1 (whether or not it also contains other regulations), the instrument may not be made unless a draft has been laid before and approved by resolution of each House of Parliament.

(4C) Subject to that, such a statutory instrument is subject to annulment in pursuance of a resolution of either House of Parliament."

PART 2

AMENDMENTS TO OTHER ACTS

National Assistance Act 1948 (c. 29)

12 (1) Section 47 of the National Assistance Act 1948 (removal to suitable premises of persons in need of care and attention) is amended as follows.

(2) After subsection (1) insert—

"(1A) But this section does not apply to a person ("P") in either of the following cases.

(1B) The first case is where an order of the Court of Protection authorises the managing authority of a hospital or care home (within the meaning of Schedule A1 to the Mental Capacity Act 2005) to provide P with proper care and attention.

(1C) The second case is where—

(a) an authorisation under Schedule A1 to the Mental Capacity Act 2005 is in force, or

(b) the managing authority of a hospital or care home are under a duty under paragraph 24 of that Schedule to request a standard authorisation, and

P is, or would be, the relevant person in relation to the authorisation."

(3) This paragraph does not extend to Scotland.

Local Authority Social Services Act 1970 (c. 42)

13 (1) Schedule 1 to the Local Authority Social Services Act 1970 (Social Services functions of local authorities) is amended as follows.

(2) In the entry relating to the Mental Capacity Act 2005 (c. 9), insert the following entries at the appropriate places—

"Section 39A	Instructing independent mental capacity advocate when giving an urgent authorisation, or making a request for a standard authorisation, under Schedule A1 to the Act."

"Section 39C	Instructing independent mental capacity advocate when no representative for relevant person under Part 10 of Schedule A1 to the Act."

"Section 39D	Instructing independent mental capacity advocate when representative for relevant person under Part 10 of Schedule A1 to the Act is not being paid."

"Schedule A1	Any functions."

SCHEDULE 10

Section 53

TRANSITIONAL PROVISIONS AND SAVINGS

Interpretation

1 (1) This Schedule is to be read as follows.

(2) Reference to an enactment is to an enactment contained in this Act, unless otherwise stated.

(3) Reference to an enactment contained in the 1983 Act includes reference to that enactment as applied by section 40(4) of that Act (patients concerned in criminal proceedings or under sentence).

Authority to detain etc

2 (1) The provisions mentioned in sub-paragraph (4) do not affect—

(a) the authority for the detention or guardianship of a person who is liable to be detained or subject to guardianship under the 1983 Act immediately before the date on which those provisions come into force,

(b) the 1983 Act in relation to any application, order or direction for admission or removal to a hospital, or any guardianship application or order, made under that Act before that date or the exercise, before that date, of any power to remand,

(c) the power to make on or after that date an application for the admission of a person to a hospital, or a guardianship application, where all the recommendations on which the application is to be founded are signed before that date, or

(d) the authority for the detention or guardianship of a person in pursuance of such an application.

(2) But those provisions do apply to the following events occurring on or after that date—

(a) any renewal of the authority for the person's detention or guardianship,

(b) any consideration of his case by a Mental Health Review Tribunal, and

(c) any decision about the exercise of any power to discharge him from detention or guardianship.

(3) Sub-paragraph (2)(b) is subject to paragraph 4.

(4) The provisions are—

(a) section 1 and Schedule 1 (removal of categories of mental disorder),

(b) section 2 (special provision for persons with learning disability),

(c) section 3 (exclusions),

(d) section 4 (replacement of "treatability" and "care" tests with appropriate treatment test),

(e) section 5 (addition of appropriate treatment test),

(f) section 7 (definition of "medical treatment"), and

(g) the repeals in Schedule 11 which are consequential on any of those sections or that Schedule.

Consent to treatment

3 (1) The amendments made by section 6 (appropriate treatment test in Part 4 of the 1983 Act) do not affect the application of a certificate under section 57(2)(b) or 58(3)(b) of the 1983 Act given before the date on which the amendments come into force.

(2) The amendments made by sections 27 and 28 (electro-convulsive therapy, etc.) do not affect the application of a certificate under subsection (3) of section 58 of the 1983 Act which—

(a) relates to electro-convulsive therapy (by virtue of regulations under subsection (1)(a) of that section), and

(b) is given before the date on which those amendments come into force.

(3) But any certificate under section 58(3)(b) of the 1983 Act that the patient has not consented to electro-convulsive therapy ceases to apply when those amendments come into force.

Reclassification of patients

4 The amendment made by paragraph 13 of Schedule 1 and the repeal in Schedule 11 of section 66(1)(d) and (fb) of the 1983 Act (which concern a patient's right to apply to a Mental Health Review Tribunal following a report about the form of his mental disorder) do not affect any right to apply in consequence of a report furnished before the date on which the amendment and repeal come into force.

Supervised community treatment

5 Section 32 and the amendments and repeals in Schedules 3 and 11 which are consequential on that section apply to a patient who is liable to be detained under the 1983 Act immediately before the date on which that section and those amendments and repeals come into force, as they apply to a patient who becomes so liable on or after that date.

Nearest relative

6 (1) Subsections (2), (3) and (4)(b) of section 23 (extension of power to appoint acting nearest relative) do not apply to the making of an order under section 29 of the 1983 Act on or after the date on which those provisions come into force, if the application for the order was made before that date.

(2) Subsections (6) and (7) of section 24 (duration of orders appointing nearest relative) do not affect—

(a) any order made under section 29 of the 1983 Act before the date on which those subsections come into force, or

(b) any order made under that section on or after that date if the application for it was made before that date.

(3) But subsections (2)(a), (4) and (5) of section 24 (applications for discharge and variation) do apply in relation to an order mentioned in sub-paragraph (2)(a) or (b).

(4) Section 25 (restriction of nearest relative's right to apply to tribunal) does not apply in relation to an order mentioned in sub-paragraph (2)(a) or (b).

7 (1) If, by virtue of section 26 (civil partners) coming into force, a person ceases to be a patient's nearest relative, this does not affect—

(a) any application to a Mental Health Review Tribunal under the 1983 Act made by that person, but not determined or withdrawn, before the date on which that section comes into force,

(b) any notice under section 25 of that Act given by that person before that date, or

(c) any application to a county court under section 30(1) of that Act made by that person, but not determined or withdrawn, before that date.

(2) But section 26 does apply to the determination on or after that date of any application under section 29 or 30 of the 1983 Act made before that date.

Independent mental health advocates

8 (1) Section 30—

(a) applies to a patient who is liable to be detained under the 1983 Act immediately before the commencement date as it applies to a patient who becomes so liable on or after that date;

(b) applies to a patient who is subject to guardianship under that Act immediately before the commencement date as it applies to a patient who becomes so subject on or after that date;

(c) applies to a patient who is a community patient under that Act immediately before the commencement date as it applies to a patient who becomes a community patient on or after that date.

(2) For the purposes of the provisions inserted by that section, a patient is to be treated as a qualifying patient within section 130C(3) of the 1983 Act if—

(a) not being a formal patient, he discussed before the commencement date with a registered medical practitioner or approved clinician the possibility of being given a form of treatment to which section 57 of that Act applies, and

(b) sub-paragraph (4) or (5) applies in relation to him.

(3) A patient is also to be treated for those purposes as a qualifying patient within section 130C(3) of the 1983 Act if—

(a) not having attained the age of 18 years and not being a formal patient, he discussed before the commencement date with a registered medical practitioner or approved clinician the possibility of being given a form of treatment to which section 58A of that Act applies, and

(b) sub-paragraph (4) or (5) applies in relation to him.

(4) This sub-paragraph applies in relation to the patient if, immediately before the commencement date, he has yet to be informed whether or not the treatment is proposed in his case.

(5) This sub-paragraph applies in relation to the patient if, immediately before the commencement date—

(a) he has been informed that the treatment is proposed in his case,

(b) the proposal has not been withdrawn, and

(c) the treatment has not been completed or discontinued.

(6) A qualifying patient in relation to whom sub-paragraph (4) applies and who is informed on or after the commencement date that the treatment is proposed in his case, or in relation to whom sub-paragraph (5) applies, remains a qualifying patient until—

(a) the proposal is withdrawn, or

(b) the treatment is completed or discontinued.

(7) In relation to a patient who is a qualifying patient within section 130C(3) of the 1983 Act by virtue of this paragraph, the responsible person under section 130D of that Act is to be the person with overall responsibility for the patient's case (and subsection (2)(e) of that section is to be read accordingly).

(8) Sub-paragraph (9) applies in relation to a patient—

(a) who is a qualifying patient within section 130C(2) of the 1983 Act by virtue of being a formal patient immediately before the commencement date, or

(b) who is a qualifying patient within section 130C(3) of that Act by virtue of this paragraph.

(9) The steps to be taken under subsection (1) of section 130D of that Act are to be taken on, or as soon as practicable after, the commencement date (and subsection (3) of that section is to be read accordingly).

(10) In this paragraph—

"approved clinician" has the same meaning as in the 1983 Act,

"the commencement date" means the date on which section 30 comes into force, and

"formal patient" means a patient who is—

(a) liable to be detained under the 1983 Act (otherwise than by virtue of section 4, 5(2) or (4), 135 or 136 of that Act),
(b) subject to guardianship under that Act, or
(c) a community patient under that Act.

Applications and references to Mental Health Review Tribunal

9 (1) The amendments made by section 37 apply in relation to a patient who is liable to be detained under the 1983 Act immediately before the date on which the amendments come into force as they apply in relation to one who becomes so liable on or after that date.

(2) The repeal in paragraph 20(b) of Schedule 3 of the reference in section 69(2)(b) of the 1983 Act to section 45B(2) of that Act (which concerns the right of a patient subject to a hospital direction to apply to a Mental Health Review Tribunal in the period of six months beginning with the date of the direction) does not affect any right to apply by virtue of a hospital direction dated before the date on which the repeal comes into force.

SCHEDULE 11

Section 55

REPEALS AND REVOCATIONS

PART 1

REMOVAL OF CATEGORIES OF MENTAL DISORDER

Reference	*Extent of repeal or revocation*
Juries Act 1974 (c. 23)	In Schedule 1, paragraph 4(1).
Mental Health Act 1983 (c. 20)	In section 1(2), the definitions of— (a) "severe mental impairment" and "severely mentally impaired", (b) "mental impairment" and "mentally impaired", and (c) "psychopathic disorder".
	In section 7(2)(a), the words ", being mental illness, severe mental impairment, psychopathic disorder or mental impairment and his mental disorder is".
	Section 11(6).
	In section 15(3), the words from "; but this subsection" to the end.
	Section 16.
	Section 20(9).
	Section 21B(8) and (9).

Reference	Extent of repeal or revocation
	In section 37— (a) in subsection (3), the words "as being a person suffering from mental illness or severe mental impairment", and (b) subsection (7).
	In section 45A, subsections (10) and (11).
	Section 47(4).
	Section 55(3).
	In section 66(1), paragraphs (d) and (fb) (and the word "or" at the end of those paragraphs).
	Section 72(5).
	Section 92(3).
	In Part 1 of Schedule 1— (a) in paragraph 2, the word "16,", (b) paragraph 3, and (c) in paragraph 6, paragraph (b) (and the word "and" immediately preceding it).
	In Schedule 5— (a) in paragraph 37(5), the words from ", and he shall be so treated" to the end, and (b) paragraph 39.
Mental Health (Patients in the Community) Act 1995 (c. 52)	In Schedule 1, paragraph 10(4).
Mental Capacity Act 2005 (c. 9)	In Schedule 4, in paragraph 23(1), the words "(within the meaning of the Mental Health Act)".
Mental Health (Care and Treatment) (Scotland) Act 2003 (Consequential Provisions) Order 2005 (S.I. 2005/2078)	In Schedule 1, paragraph 2(8).

PART 2

REPLACEMENT OF "TREATABILITY" AND "CARE" TESTS

Reference	Extent of repeal or revocation
Mental Health Act 1983 (c. 20)	In section 3(2), paragraph (b) (and the word "and" at the end of that paragraph).
	In section 20(4)— (a) paragraph (b) (and the word "and" at the end of that paragraph), and (b) the words from "but, in the case of mental illness" to the end.

Reference	*Extent of repeal or revocation*
	Section 72(2).

PART 3

APPROVED CLINICIANS AND RESPONSIBLE CLINICIANS

Reference	*Extent of repeal or revocation*
Mental Health Act 1983 (c. 20)	Section 20(10).
	In section 21B(10), the definition of "appropriate medical officer".
	In section 61(3), the words "to the responsible medical officer".
Health and Social Care (Community Health and Standards) Act 2003 (c. 43)	In Schedule 4, paragraph 51.
Civil Partnership Act 2004 (c. 33)	In Schedule 27, paragraph 86(a).
National Health Service (Consequential Provisions) Act 2006 (c. 43)	In Schedule 1, paragraph 63.

PART 4

SAFEGUARDS FOR PATIENTS

Reference	*Extent of repeal or revocation*
Mental Health Act 1983	In section 29— (a) in subsection (2), the words from "but in relation to" to the end, and (b) in subsection (3), the word "or" at the end of paragraph (c).

PART 5

SUPERVISED COMMUNITY TREATMENT

Reference	*Extent of repeal or revocation*
Mental Health Act 1983	In section 18(4), the words from "and, in determining" to the end.
	Sections 25A to 25J.
	In section 29(3)(d), the words "from hospital or guardianship".
	In section 32(2)(c), the words "or to after-care under supervision".

Reference	Extent of repeal or revocation
	In section 34— (a) in subsection (1), the definitions of "the community responsible medical officer" and "the supervisor", and (b) subsection (1A).
	In section 66(1)— (a) paragraphs (ga), (gb) and (gc) (and the word "or" at the end of each of those paragraphs), and (b) in sub-paragraph (i), the words from "or, in the cases" to the end.
	In section 66(2)— (a) in paragraph (d), the words "and (gb)", and (b) paragraph (fa).
	In section 67(1), the words "or to after-care under supervision".
	In section 69(2)(b), the words "45B(2), 46(3),".
	Section 72(4A).
	In section 76(1), the words from "or to after-care" to "leaves hospital)".
	Section 117(2A).
	Section 127(2A).
	In section 145— (a) in subsection (1), the definitions of "the responsible after-care bodies" and "supervision application", and (b) subsection (1A).
	In section 146, the words from "128" to "guardianship)".
	In Part 1 of Schedule 1— (a) in paragraph 2, the words ", 25A, 25B", and (b) paragraph 8A.
Mental Health (Patients in the Community) Act 1995 (c. 52)	Section 1(1).
	In Schedule 1— (a) in paragraph 2, paragraph (c) (and the word "and" immediately preceding it), (b) in paragraph 11, paragraph (a) (and the word "and" at the end of that paragraph), and (c) paragraphs 3, 4, 6, 7, 8(2), 10(1) to (3), 12, 13, 18 and 20.

Reference	*Extent of repeal or revocation*
Crime (Sentences) Act 1997 (c. 43)	In Schedule 4, paragraph 12(8).
National Health Service Reform and Health Care Professions Act 2002 (c. 17)	In Schedule 2, paragraphs 43 to 45.
Civil Partnership Act 2004 (c. 33)	In Schedule 27, in paragraph 86, paragraph (b) (and the word "and" immediately preceding it).

PART 6

ORGANISATION OF TRIBUNALS

Reference	*Extent of repeal or revocation*
Mental Health Act 1983 (c. 20)	In section 78(6), the words ", if for any reason he is unable to act,".
	In section 143(2), the words "or 65".
	In paragraph 4 of Schedule 2, the words ", if for any reason he is unable to act,".
Health Authorities Act 1995 (c. 17)	In Schedule 1, paragraph 107(13).

PART 7

CROSS-BORDER ARRANGEMENTS

Reference	*Extent of repeal or revocation*
Mental Health Act 1983	In section 80(1), the words "or subject to guardianship" and the words "or, as the case may be, for receiving him into guardianship".
	In section 88(3)— (a) the words "to Scotland or Northern Ireland", (b) paragraph (a), and (c) in paragraph (b), the words "in Northern Ireland,".
	In section 146, the words from "88" to "138)".
Mental Health (Care and Treatment) (Scotland) Act 2003 (Consequential Provisions) Order 2005 (S.I. 2005/2078)	Articles 1(5), 2 and 3.
	In Schedule 1, paragraph 2(5).

PART 8

RESTRICTED PATIENTS

Reference	*Extent of repeal or revocation*
Colonial Prisoners Removal Act 1884 (c. 31)	In section 10(3)(a), the words ", made without limitation of time".
Mental Health Act 1983	In section 41(1), the words ", either without limit of time or during such period as may be specified in the order".
	In section 42(4)(b), the words from ", and, if the restriction order was made for a specified period," to the end.
	In section 44(3), the words ", made without limitation of time".
	In section 81(7), the words "restriction order or" in each place,
	In section 81A(3)— (a) the words "restriction order or" in each place, and (b) the words "order or".
	In section 84(2), the words ", made without limitation of time".
	In section 91(2), the words "at any time before the end of the period for which those orders would have continued in force".

PART 9

MISCELLANEOUS

Reference	*Extent of repeal or revocation*
Children Act 1989 (c. 41)	In Schedule 13, paragraph 48(5).

PART 10

DEPRIVATION OF LIBERTY

Reference	*Extent of repeal or revocation*
Mental Capacity Act 2005 (c. 9)	Section 6(5).
	Section 11(6).
	Section 20(13).

Adapted and published by GRANGIS under the OGL Licence 3.0.

www.nationalarchives.gov.uk/doc/open-government-licence/version/3/

GRANGIS - UK PUBLISHING 2022.

Thank you for taking the time to leave us a review regarding this version

★★★★★

For further inquiries, contact us at:
www.grangis.com / contact@grangis.com

www.ingramcontent.com/pod-product-compliance
Lightning Source LLC
LaVergne TN
LVHW060212210926
848481LV00008B/2707
9798885590280